D1602114

The Masculinity Manifesto

THE MASCULINITY MANIFESTO

HOW A MAN ESTABLISHES INFLUENCE, CREDIBILITY & AUTHORITY

RYAN MICHLER

SALEM
BOOKS
an imprint of Regnery Publishing
Washington, D.C.

Salem Books™ is a trademark of Salem Communications Holding Corporation. Regnery® is a registered trademark and its colophon is a trademark of Salem Communications Holding Corporation.

ISBN: 978-1-68451-331-4
eISBN: 978-1-68451-344-4

Library of Congress Control Number: 2022941037

Published in the United States by
Salem Books
An Imprint of Regnery Publishing
A Division of Salem Media Group
Washington, D.C.
www.SalemBooks.com

Manufactured in the United States of America

10 9 8 7 6 5 4 3 2 1

Books are available in quantity for promotional or premium use. For information on discounts and terms, please visit our website: www.SalemBooks.com.

To my beautiful wife, Tricia, my three incredible sons, and my lovely daughter. I will never lose focus and I will never jeopardize my priorities. You are the reason for my work and the fuel for the words found in this book.

CONTENTS

CONTENTS

Part III

HARNESS MASCULINITY FOR PRODUCTIVE OUTCOMES 87

Part IV

LIVE LIKE A MAN 187

INTRODUCTION

In 2015, I started a fledgling little podcast called *Order of Man*. Since then, that podcast has been downloaded more than forty-five million times, has grown its reach across various social media platforms to more than a million followers, and I can't even count how many men have messaged us with sincere gratitude for the work we've been doing over the past seven years.

But truth be told, I didn't set out to reach millions of men across the world. I didn't set out to record more than nine hundred episodes as of 2021, over four hundred of them with some of the most influential men on the planet: Tim Tebow, Terry Crews, Matthew McConaughey, Jocko Willink, Dave Ramsey, David Goggins, Ben Shapiro, Andy Frisella, Tim Kennedy, Dan Crenshaw, and so many others.

No, I started it with much different, more selfish intentions. I simply wanted to learn how to become a more capable man. Period, end of story (or so I thought). There were men I followed whom I wanted to learn from. But as a relative nobody, very few of those men would give me the time of day, let alone offer me any sort of personalized one-on-one coaching.

At the time, I already had a podcast called *Wealth Anatomy*. It was something I began in order to pick up new clients in my relatively successful financial planning practice. But if I'm being honest, I was getting tired of talking with my clients about money. I would look down at my phone when a client called and dread answering it. I really enjoyed the relationships I had with my clients, but I was done talking about investments, insurance, and retirement planning.

I figured that since I enjoyed the medium of podcasting (although I was ready for a different type of conversation), maybe I could convince some of the men who inspired me to join me in recording a brief conversation. That way, I would get personalized coaching, and they would get access to my nonexistent audience (sounds like quite the deal, right?).

Well, it worked. And, since you're reading a copy of this book, you might have benefited from that humble little podcast that started in 2015.

That said, not a day goes by that I don't feel like I'm the greatest recipient of the work my team and I do here. Each day, I get to talk with some of the most successful men out there; work closely with the thousands of men who are currently in or have gone through our programs, courses, and events; and interact with you and the rest of the men who are inspired and edified by the work we're doing to reclaim and restore masculinity.

Over the past seven years, I've learned a lot about what it means to be a man. But that sentiment seems to escape a lot of people in modern times. Frequently, I meet anonymous strangers on the interwebs who seem to believe that "any man who has to *learn* to be a man is no man at all."

That isn't true. Not even close. If you're talking about being *male*, sure, but a *man*, no. Where being a male is a matter of birthright, being a man is earned. I've spent countless hours talking with others, researching, unpacking, and working toward becoming more of a man myself. Through my work, I've discovered some incredibly powerful concepts regarding masculinity and manliness that modern culture generally rejects.

And that's exactly what you're going to find within the pages of this book. We're going to explore what masculinity is, what it means to be a man, what men do, and the path to fulfillment for men.

Now, inevitably, when I dare attempt to describe masculinity and what it means to be a man, I'm often met with comments like, "What makes you qualified to tell others what it means to be a man?" The simple answer is this: I have a willingness and desire to do so. That's it. I'm on the path. I've never once asserted that I know more than any other man or that I am the epitome of masculinity.

In fact, I'm still very inadequate in many ways. And, not too long ago, you'd hardly even recognize me. Thirteen years ago, I was a shell of the man that I am today. My wife had just left me with our one-year-old son, my financial planning practice was struggling (I was very close to throwing in the towel), and I weighed fifty pounds more than I do today. I was broke—mentally, physically, emotionally, and spiritually.

It was, without a doubt, the darkest time in my life. Slowly and gradually, I began to pull myself out of the pit of despair I had personally dug. I built a band of brothers, I hired mentors, I listened to every self-help CD and read every self-help book I could get my hands on. Things began to change, and the trajectory I put myself on is what led me to this work.

I don't share this with you to beat my chest. I look around and hear from men who are not only hurting mentally, physically, emotionally, and spiritually (as I was) but struggling at the core with who they are as men, and I can't help but feel an immense sense of obligation to share what I've been blessed to learn.

Through my work, I've been able to pull back the curtain, so to speak, to see not only what makes men tick but what attributes, skills, and characteristics lead them down a path of satisfaction and fulfillment. And isn't that what we're all after?

I'd contend that we, as men, are not after "happiness," as so many claim. After all, happiness, to me, represents a state of ignorant bliss free from headache, heartache, and hardship.

No, that isn't what we're after. We want to feel useful, productive, and valuable, or what I describe as *fulfilled*. And fulfillment does not come from the absence of challenge and adversity (happiness), but from the ability to overcome it effectively. In fact, fulfillment can come from some of the most trying times we've ever faced.

In 2017, I wrote a book titled *Sovereignty: The Battle for the Hearts and Minds of Men*. In it, I asserted that in order for a man to be fulfilled, he must first learn to lead himself well. In that book, I articulated the path men need to follow to reclaim their lives and take control of their own destinies. At the time, I saw too many men relinquishing autonomy and control over their lives to their wives or girlfriends, children, employers, and government. While I would still agree that the *first* step to fulfillment is realizing and harnessing the power a man has over his own life, I now see that it is only *part* of the process.

The next evolution is to learn how to take your newly earned sovereignty and turn it outward so that you can effectively lead others well. We, after all, are designed biologically, not societally, to lead (more on that later). Imagine with me, for a minute, a life in which you, as a man, have the confidence you've dreamed of. Your wife looks at you with adoration in her eyes. Your children cling to your words and example. They ask for your advice, follow your direction, and live their lives in your footsteps before feeling empowered to create their own. Your employees are honored to work with you and consider it a privilege to learn from you. Your neighbors and acquaintances turn to you for guidance, direction, and assistance. You are loved and valued inside the walls of your home and business and within the borders of your neighborhood and community.

I can't deny that even I, a man who has dedicated his life to studying and applying masculinity, get a little choked up when I imagine the life I just cast before you.

If you're anything like me and that vision of a fulfilled life speaks to you, you're in the right place. You picked up the right book. You need to know that a fulfilled life isn't some utopian dream available only to a select few. It's available to every man who learns what it takes to make it so.

And I'm going to help you do it. "Why me?" you might ask. Because I know what it's like to live a life that is the antithesis of a fulfilled one. And I know what needs to happen to pull yourself from the depths of despair or, at a minimum, from a deep, unyielding sense of inadequacy. I am not that special. There is nothing particularly unique about me. I stumble like any man. I've made more mistakes than I care to admit. I've hurt people—even those I love the most—more than I can ever make amends for. In spite of all that, I've built a tremendously fulfilling life for myself and those I care about most.

With all that said, if you believe, like me, that the ultimate objective is to live a life of fulfillment and you can see, at least to some degree, that proper leadership (service to others) is the path to get there, the question that begs answering is, "How do we then lead more effectively?"

The answer to that question is the purpose of this book. It's to show you as a husband, father, business owner, community leader, politician, pastor, team leader, project manager, etc., how to foster influence, credibility, and authority—the brickwork of effective leadership, which inevitably leads to a life of fulfillment.

But before we get started, what you need to know is that there are forces at work against you. If this were a seamless path, you'd see more men walking on it. You don't, for a reason. There are both external (societal) and internal (emotional) factors at play that cause many men to reject the path they're meant to walk, and then ultimately, slip into a life of complacency, underperformance, and despair.

So, to start this journey, we're going to discuss what it means to be a man in the first place. You can't lead others effectively and reach the level of fulfillment you desire if you don't know who you are and who you're meant to be. That's the focus of Part I: "Bear the Burden." The work of men isn't comfortable or convenient. But anything worth pursuing never is. We'll talk about what makes a man a man, the archetypes of manliness, and why developing influence, authority, and credibility is crucial to men.

In Part II: "The Mindsets of Masculine Leadership," we'll explore four unique mentalities that effective, competent men operate by:

- Overcome the Ease of Modernity
- Don't Be a Superhero
- Lead before the Title
- Render Yourself Obsolete

You'll also uncover how so many notions of "modern masculinity" are counterproductive and don't lead to a life of fulfillment at all, as they claim, but rather a life of missed opportunities and unrealized potential.

And, in Part III: "Harness Masculinity for Productive Outcomes," you'll be introduced to eight specific masculine virtues defined not by society but by biology:

- Stoicism
- Competitiveness
- Dominance
- Aggression
- Vigilance
- Violence
- Honesty
- Self-Respect

You will be challenged to implement these virtues in your life for productive outcomes for you, your family, and society as a whole. While much of society would have you silence the virtues we unpack in Part III, I will call you to lean into and harness them. People don't follow watered-down versions of men. They do, however, follow those with influence, credibility, and authority. You'll learn how to establish all three.

With the knowledge found in this book, I'll help you set the record straight about what it means to be a man and to fight our natural tendency to take the path of least resistance. More importantly, I'll equip you with the mindset and framework required to live a life fulfilled.

If you're looking for an easy path or the "three-part formula for success," I'd suggest you close this book, put it down, and concern yourself with finding "happiness." But if living your life as a man is what you're after, brace yourself, open your mind and heart, and prepare to do the work.

Ready? Begin.

PART I

BEAR THE BURDEN

It's in responsibility that most people find the meaning that sustains them through life. It's not in happiness. It's not in impulsive pleasure.

—Jordan Peterson

I've never been one to mince words. It's served me well in my life, but at times, I've been known to stick my foot in my mouth. That said, it's crucial that you understand something about the journey you're about to embark upon: It's a burden. It isn't easy.

Sure, I could sugarcoat it and pretend that this is a book about making you feel better about yourself and your current choices. But I don't think you would have picked up a copy if all you wanted was to hear how good you already are and that you're doing all the things you should be doing.

The truth is that you're not. You know it. I know it. There is no escaping it. Well, actually there is one way to escape it—start doing the things you know you should. We're going to get to that, but before we do, you need to understand who you are as a man, what you're capable of, and what stands in your way. And there is plenty standing in your way—both internally and externally.

But know that I don't consider it my job, nor do I think it's possible, to eliminate all the factors keeping you from becoming the man you're meant to be. That said, it is possible to make yourself capable of overcoming them—to bear the burden of masculinity. It's like Bruce Lee said: "Do not pray for an easy life; pray for the strength to endure a difficult one."

So let's talk about why you should consider "bearing the burden," and what that burden even is.

As I type this, I'm reminded of one of the most memorable and impactful days of my life: March 25, 2008. My wife had just informed me that she was having serious contractions and was ready to go to the hospital to deliver our first baby. I wasn't ready (as if "ready" is even possible as a first-time father). She was four weeks ahead of schedule. I'd thought I had plenty of time; God had different plans for us.

Frantically, I threw our bags in the car and raced to the hospital. After a few hours, the nurses informed us that my wife wasn't dilated to the point where she was ready to deliver. False alarm . . . or so it would seem.

Disappointed, we drove home. After sleeping for a few hours, my wife again notified me, "The doctors were wrong. It's time to go—now!"

Again, we drove to the hospital. This time, the nurses agreed with my wife and admitted her immediately. I can't quite remember the range of emotions I experienced that day, but I do know that I've never prayed to God as deeply as I did then.

"I'm not ready, God."

"I'm not capable of caring for this child."

"I don't know how to do this."

"I'm scared."

Then, my line of pleas began to change. They changed from fears of inadequacy to requests for strength.

"God, please help me be a good father."

"Give me the strength to raise my son well."

"Help me to do Your will as I raise him."

Believe me, that is not an insignificant change in thinking. The first line of thinking is one of paralysis. Those are incomplete thoughts. "I'm not ready" is an insufficient sentence. It does nothing to lead a man toward action. In fact, if anything, it stalemates progress. "I'm not ready. Period," as in "End of story. End of discussion."

But that isn't the end of discussion, is it? "I'm not ready yet" is closer to complete. "I'm not ready yet, therefore, I am going to . . ." is even better.

In that cold hospital room the morning of March 26, 2008, I began to realize that although I was flooded with a sense of inadequacy, I suspected that I could indeed become capable of raising this little human.

Are you willing to complete the sentence? Are you willing to do your duty as a man? Are you willing to do what is necessary to bear the burden of masculinity?

I ask this because, unless you're ready, you'll always shirk your responsibility and slink your way into obscurity. That's the easy way that so many men have chosen to take. That isn't the call to bear the burden, but the antithesis of it. Unless you're ready, you'll always hear the looming question in your mind, as John Eldredge stated in his book *Wild at Heart*, "Do I have what it takes?"

Do you? I don't know. Neither do you. But in this book, I'm going to challenge you to find out.

When I was a young boy, I would read Choose Your Own Adventure books. If you remember, the reader was instructed to read a few pages before being presented with a choice between two or more options. If option A was chosen, the reader was directed to page 2. If option B was chosen, he was directed to page 7.

I'm asking you to make a decision today.

Do you choose the path of least resistance? It's likely the one that you're currently on. Do you resign yourself to incomplete thoughts like "I am not enough"? Do you submit to your current circumstances, throw up your hands, and convince yourself that nothing can be done?

Or do you choose to finish the sentence: "I am not enough *yet*, therefore I will bear the burden of responsibility"?

One last thing before we move on: The reason I shared the story of my first son's birth is because, perhaps for the first time in my life, that's when I began to realize what it meant to be a man and what burden I was meant to carry. Let me be clear: You do not have to father and raise children in order to call yourself a man, but you *do* have to accept and make yourself capable of bearing a meaningful burden. Unfortunately, up to the point of having my first son, I was playing the part of a man, but I wasn't *being* a man. After all, a man really isn't a man at all until he's fulfilling a purpose and capable of being of service to others. That's the burden. It is one worth bearing well.

CHAPTER ONE

WHAT MAKES A MAN A MAN

I mean to make myself a man, and if I succeed in that,
I shall succeed in everything else.

—*James A. Garfield*

All right, so let's talk about what makes a man a man. There is a dangerous misconception among many that being a man is a birthright. It isn't.

A male? Yes. A man? No.

The simple truth of the matter is that being a male is a matter of biology. Being a man, however, is so much more than that. Simply put, what defines a man is his ability to harness his birthright (maleness) toward productive outcomes for himself, his loved ones, and those for whom he has a responsibility (manliness).

Take my three sons as an example. They are male. No doubt about it. It is scientifically factual. Are they men? Of course not. No one even expects them to be. Suffice it to say that the reason we don't consider my fourteen-, eleven-, and six-year-old sons to be men is because they are not mature enough to harness the raw masculinity that courses through their veins. They're temperamental. They're irrational. They're overly emotional. And they have no way of providing for themselves. In other words, they're dependent.

But is that any different from the thirty- and forty-year-old men we see still living in Mommy and Daddy's basement? No, it really isn't. Barring mental illness, a thirty-five-year-old male living with his parents has all the mental, emotional, and physical capacity to become a man, yet he chooses not to. And that's the difference. It's a choice. You, as my friend Jack Donovan would say, have to choose to be a man.

That's why manliness has less to do with age and more to do with the choices you make on a daily basis as a male.

I'm reminded of a story about a fifteen-year-old young man named Joseph Lodge. In 1863, at the age of fifteen, he left his home in search of work after his father died, leaving his mother and siblings without any income.

He traveled to Illinois, Wisconsin, Iowa, Missouri, and Louisiana, looking for work. For most of the time, he traveled on foot. In one of his journal excerpts from 1867, he shared, "Start this morning in a light rain with mud half up to my knees. Travel about 18 miles and the rain compels me to stop for my feet have been wet all day as I was compelled to wade in Coons River which was over my boot tops with ice water mostly."

Later that year, in October 1867, he boarded a ship to Cuba, eventually making his way to Peru, where he built and operated railroads and would send money back to his mother and siblings.

He continued to travel for the next thirty years, mostly managing blast furnaces and coal mines until establishing Blacklock Foundry to manufacture soil pipe. In 1910, Blacklock Foundry burned to the ground, which led him to rebuild it only a few blocks away, naming it Lodge Manufacturing Company.[1]

One hundred twenty-five years later, the Lodge Manufacturing Company stands as a testament to what a young boy who decided to be a man in the face of tremendous adversity can create.

It's hard to imagine a fifteen-year-old boy today leaving home to pay his mother's and siblings' bills when the reality is that he is likely more interested in the latest video game or proliferation of accessible pornography and more consumed with pleasing himself than worrying about those around him.

Yet here we are, wondering where all the "real men" have gone.

Look, it's crucial we make the distinction between "male" and "man," because unless a male knows who he is meant to be as a man, he will inevitably live a life less than he is capable of. Let's take, for example, suicide rates among men. Recent studies have suggested that it is nearly four times higher than those of women.

The Doctrine of Popular Culture would suggest that the reason we see such levels of depression and suicide in men is because they've bought into "dangerous gender ideologies" and "traditional gender norms" that have hurt and hindered them. I, however, would contend that the reason we see a higher rate of suicide in men is because we've moved away from those roles in exchange for something significantly more self-absorbed and, not coincidentally, less meaningful.

See, much of modern culture has bought into the notion that masculinity is a societal construct. It isn't. It's a biological construct supported societally, for good reason: it works. It really wasn't until the relative ease of modernity that we even had the luxury of calling into question what makes a man a man.

The great Roman emperor and stoic philosopher Marcus Aurelius once said, "Waste no more time arguing about what a good man should be. Be one."

That was nearly two thousand years ago. And I don't need to remind you that two thousand years ago, we didn't have vehicles, cell phones, super computers, and social media, all of which have made life just a bit easier, improved our standard of living, and drastically extended our life expectancy from roughly twenty to thirty-three years in ancient Rome to over seventy-eight years in 2021.

So, two thousand years ago, a male had less of a choice to make than he does today: be a man or die.

Whenever I broach this subject, I'm often met with, "Ryan, the world has changed. It's not necessary to attach ourselves to archaic definitions of masculinity." While I can certainly agree that the world is a safer, less hostile place than it was two thousand or even two hundred years ago, it doesn't render the role of men or even masculinity useless or unnecessary.

In fact, it's quite the opposite. A male who knows who he is and who he has the potential to become is far more likely to live a life of purpose and meaning. And because he lives a life of purpose and meaning, he is far more likely to apply his unique and biological attributes in constructive ways to the world around him. The alternative—buying into the idea that a man just is, not who he can become—leads to nihilism.

In a world where *my* truth has replaced *the* truth, vulnerability and victimhood are viewed as strength, men can be women and vice versa, and absolutely nothing means anything, is it any wonder we see so many men confused by and frustrated with the discrepancy between who the world tells them they are and who they actually believe themselves to be?

If you're anything like me, you feel it. You know deep down inside that you are destined for something more. You're right. You are. You are called to be a man. Whether you accept that calling is a choice you'll have to make.

But I can promise you this: if you do decide to accept the calling, the people you love and care for will begin to see you in a different light because *you* see you in a different light.

Knowing that you are a man (or can become one), and that "man" actually means something, is the foundation for establishing and leading with influence, credibility, and authority. In fact, a male is viewed as a man only when he is making himself capable of doing so.

CHAPTER TWO

THE ARCHETYPE OF MANLINESS: PROTECT, PROVIDE, PRESIDE

The real man gains renown by standing between his family and destruction, absorbing the blows of fate with equanimity.

—David Gilmore

In his book *Manhood in the Making: Cultural Concepts of Masculinity*, anthropologist David Gilmore introduces us to the idea that masculinity is not a "societal construct" as so many like to claim.[1] If it were a societal construct, it would be difficult, if not impossible, to explain why nearly every culture (many of which have never been introduced to each other) have such striking similarities in their perception of masculinity and manliness.

No, masculinity is *not* constructed societally. It is constructed *biologically*. Whether you're a creationist, evolutionist, or somewhere in between, there is a reason that so many cultures view males through the lens of these biological constructs: they work for society as a whole.

In their research from August 2011, Yanna J. Weisberg, Colin G. DeYoung, and Jacob B. Hirsh discovered and articulated the differences between men and women in the Big Five personality traits. They found that women, when it comes to Neuroticism, generally score higher, with the exception of factors like anger or hostility. This makes sense. Men are generally more prone to protection and defense. When it comes to Agreeableness, which is defined as a "tendency toward cooperation, maintenance of social harmony," consideration of others, and similar measures such as tender-mindedness, women generally score higher than men. Again, this makes sense. We typically view women as more empathetic and nurturing in their roles than their counterparts. When it comes to Extraversion (which is linked to sensitivity and rewards), women generally score higher in Warmth, Gregariousness, and Positive Emotions, whereas men tend to score higher on Assertiveness and Excitement. And when it comes to Openness/Intellect, women generally score higher on the facets of Aesthetics and Feelings as opposed to men, who score higher on the Ideas facet. The only exception in the Big Five is Conscientiousness (which comprises traits related to self-discipline, organization, and control of impulses), where no significant gender difference was found.[2]

These findings seem to support Gilmore's assertion that manliness, although often believed to be constructed and supported by a society's values, is actually constructed in our biological differences (not to mention the differences in size, strength, and physical capacity between genders). In his findings, Gilmore asserts that manhood throughout the cultures he studied can be narrowed down to three *P*s: protect, provide, and procreate.

I agree that protecting and providing are objective hallmarks of manliness, but I disagree with the third, procreating. I'm sure we all know males whom we consider men who have neither the capacity nor the desire to father children. That's why I don't consider *procreation* to be the third archetype of manliness. Instead, I believe *preside* (to be in the position of authority) replaces it. After all, isn't effective fatherhood an aspect of one who presides or a potential role he could fulfill?

All that is to say that what defines a man is his ability to protect, provide, and preside. A man is not defined by what he thinks, his intentions, and/or what he hopes to accomplish someday. A man *is* defined by what he does or, more accurately, what he produces.

In his book *Wild at Heart*, John Eldredge says, "Deep in his heart, every man longs for a battle to fight, an adventure to live, and a beauty to rescue." It happens to be one of my favorite quotes because it perfectly encapsulates the three archetypes of masculinity:

A battle to fight = protect

An adventure to live = preside

A beauty to rescue = provide

That notion that a man is defined by what many call "archaic constraints" isn't as popular as it once was. Increasingly, men are told they can be anything they want to be. While I agree that there are an infinite number of ways a man can fulfill the archetypes of masculinity, there are *only* three that truly define who he is. Anything less than actively working toward making yourself capable of fulfilling these roles makes you less of a man.

Now, before anyone gets up in arms about my calling someone less of a man, please allow me to make my case.

PROTECTOR

The first archetype of manliness is that of the protector. It is biologically hardwired into who we are. I already explained the differences in the Big Five personality traits and how they lead us as men to increased aggression, violence, and anger, but let's break it down even further. Let's look at which hormones, specifically, cause us to act and react the way we do: testosterone and vasopressin.

In her book *The Male Brain*, Dr. Louann Brizendine describes testosterone as

> Zeus. King of male hormones, he is dominant, aggressive, and all-powerful. Focused and goal oriented, he feverishly builds all that is male, including the compulsion to outrank other males in the pecking order. He drives the masculine sweat glands to produce the come-hither smell of manhood—androstenedione. He activates the sex and aggression circuits, and he's single-minded in his dogged pursuit of

his desired mate. Prized for confidence and bravery, he can be
a convincing seducer, but when he's irritable, he can be the
grouchiest of bears.[3]

Next is vasopressin, which plays a crucial role in defensive behavior
and that of a protector. Although females also produce vasopressin (along
with testosterone), "the actual physiological effects of vasopressin support physical mobilization and defensive aggression, which may be critical in male mammals."[4]

There is zero doubt that men are quite literally designed to protect. The hormones testosterone and vasopressin, among others, are
proof that we aren't just encouraged by members of society to protect,
but that the role of protector is biologically built in.

On a more anecdotal level, my wife often jokingly mocks my
posture and demeanor when in unfamiliar public places. She says,
"You puff up, lift your shoulders, and give off a general 'f*** off'
attitude."

It's not as if I deliberately and intentionally deploy these tactics. I
don't think back to the days when my mother, father, schoolteacher,
coach, etc., sat me down and said, "Ryan, in order to ward off predators,
lift your shoulders, attempt to make yourself appear bigger than you
actually are, and stare menacingly at any would-be adversary." No, I
don't give it a second thought—and yet I do it. So do you, whether you
realize it or not.

The reason is that you're a protector—or at least you're designed to
be one. As I will continue to prove throughout this book, a man who
more fully embraces his natural role will inevitably find more fulfillment
in his life.

PROVIDER

In March 2008, I became a first-time father. As I mentioned before,
my son was born four weeks early. I vividly remember the day my wife

and I walked out of that hospital, completely unprepared and unqualified to be parents.

For the first few weeks of my son's life, he had to spend twenty-plus hours in what could only be described as a "briefcase tanning bed" because his liver had not fully developed. Although we were glad he didn't have to spend any time in the neonatal intensive care unit, we struggled knowing that his body wasn't completely working as it should.

I remember a lot of sleepless nights lying in front of the neon lights of that tanning bed. I would take a two- to four-hour shift in the living room with our newborn son before trading my wife the couch for the comfort of our bed.

But I also remember feeling something on those sleepless nights that I have never before felt in my life. It was a deepened sense of responsibility I had never experienced before.

That deepened sense of responsibility led to some of the darkest times of my life. There were days I would come home to my wife and son frustrated and exhausted that I had not been able to make a sale in my financial planning practice. I quite literally wore a dirt path in our grass in the backyard as I paced back and forth, stressing over how I would make the mortgage payment.

Although I don't wish those days on any of my brothers, it illustrates perfectly our role of provider and how we feel when we consider ourselves inadequate to provide for those for whom we are responsible.

That's a major distinction between what it means to be a male and what it means to be a man. Simply put, a boy consumes more than he produces; a man produces more than he consumes.

Is it really any wonder, then, that an adult male feels so sorry for himself when he has proven that not only can he not take care of himself, but that he has zero capacity to take care of others? Unfortunately, when so many males come to that realization, instead of embracing the challenge of providing in abundance, they turn to drugs, alcohol, pornography, gambling, womanizing, or anything else that may distract themselves from their own inadequacy.

Alternatively, consider the deep sense of joy, satisfaction, and pride that comes from knowing that not only can you take care of yourself, but you can take care of you and yours. Only then can you really call yourself a provider.

PRESIDER

Every man wants to lead. That may not be true in every single capacity (father, husband, boss, preacher, coach, mentor, counselor, team leader, etc.), but there is zero doubt that we all want to lead in one form or another. Is that because we were conditioned to lead by those closest to us, or is that because leadership calls to us as some unrecognizable force we may or may not have acknowledged yet?

I'd argue that it's the latter.

But there is a problem. There's another, often unrecognizable force at play: the natural man. The natural man is the weaker, lesser, more pathetic version of yourself. The natural man wants the results without the effort. He'll lie, cheat, and steal if he can get away with it. He's lazy, cowardly, selfish, and seeks immediate gratification.

That's the antithesis of what it means to preside. A man who presides values honor, integrity, and selfless service. A man who presides can not only see further than others can, but he can stay in the fight longer that most are willing to. He puts himself at risk for the greater good and recognizes that although he is at the helm, it is not all about him.

If you're anything like me, that sends a chill down your spine. You recognize it. You feel it. It may be hard to articulate, but you know it's there, don't you?

All anyone is waiting on is for you to step up and answer the call. That's the interesting thing about leadership. Every man wants to lead; few are willing to do anything about it.

Desire is fleeting. It ebbs and flows with convenience. Genuine leadership, however, isn't driven by desire alone but by selfless service to something greater than any one man. In alignment with the other arche-types of masculinity, it requires not only your birthright (maleness) but your ability to harness it (manliness).

You, as the man, are the one who is called to lead. We've already discussed through our explanation of the Big Five personality traits and the hormones coursing through your veins (testosterone and vasopressin among others) why that's the case.

But consider what happens when shit hits the proverbial fan:

In an active shooter situation, who do people look to? The man.

When the marriage begins to fall apart, who is expected to fix it? The man.

When the finances are getting out of hand, who steps in and steps up? The man.

When something needs to get done, who does it? The man.

Does that mean that women are incapable of leading? Of course not. It only goes to show that men are primed to lead. The only question that remains is, are you willing and capable of doing so?

THE WELL-ROUNDED MAN

I've found that many men are exceptionally dialed in on one arche-type at the expense of the others. But if we leave room on the table when it comes to how we harness our masculinity, we may find ourselves inadequately prepared when a situation presents itself.

For example, if you're great at providing income for your family without the ability to provide the emotional and mental support your children need, can you really say that you're fulfilling your duty as a father? Partially? Yes. Fully? No.

If you have shaped yourself into a deadly weapon, the epitome of the masculine physique, and have become an expert in the use of weapons to protect yourself and others but you can't feed or clothe your family, can you stare confidently in the mirror at the one who is looking back?

If you can lead a team of dozens or thousands but you crumble when confronted with violence, are you really any sort of leader at all? No, of course not.

Therefore, it isn't your ability to become proficient in only one or two of the archetypes of masculinity, but to become well-rounded in all three, that defines who you are and how you feel about yourself. When you learn to round out your performance, you will become confident in not only who you are as a male but who you are as a man.

To do that, you're going to have to learn to play well with others (easier for some of us than for others). The truth is, we don't live in a vacuum, and, contrary to popular belief among many men, the "lone wolf" mentality will only get you so far.

Frankly, it's impossible to walk through life without having to interact with others. Why would you want to, anyway? Talk about a miserable existence. But that doesn't mean it's always going to be easy. And it doesn't mean people will always pay us the respect we believe we deserve. But if we have any hope of fulfilling our own desires and helping others fulfill theirs, we'll have to learn to garner influence, authority, and credibility with others. After all, your family, friends, neighbors, colleagues, coworkers, etc., do get a say in the matter. Let's talk about it . . .

CHAPTER THREE

INFLUENCE, AUTHORITY, AND CREDIBILITY

Think twice before you speak, because your words and influence will plant the seed of either success or failure in the mind of another.

—*Napoleon Hill*

I know what many men think when they hear the words "influence," "authority," and "credibility." Many of them seem to believe that because a man is working to establish any of these three that he must be doing it at the expense of others. Quite the opposite, actually. Influence, authority, and credibility must be earned and verified through the acknowledgment of others. Without that acknowledgment, there is no hope in leading others effectively.

That's not to say that we should be seeking the acknowledgment or validation of others. We shouldn't. Or, at a minimum, we should be *selective* about whose affirmation we're seeking. It would be a mistake for me to ignore feedback from my wife, children, employees, etc. They are the people who will be most impacted by the decisions I make. If I would like them to buy into the vision I cast and the directives I give, it would be in all of our best interests for me to ensure that they acknowledge me as a man who is capable of leading them well. If they don't, that indicates I still have work to do.

I imagine that most of our trepidation when it comes to leading others stems from either a negative experience we had with someone we trusted or the general cultural perception of the "tyrannical patriarchy" in which we live. There is growing sentiment in modern culture that the success of one person (or a group of people) can be attributed solely to *power* (another word which has negative connotations) dynamics as opposed to *capability* dynamics.

Look, I'm not here to suggest that people who would centralize power at the expense of others don't exist. We all know they do. I could write a never-ending volume of books highlighting those who have committed horrible atrocities throughout history in their quest to do just that.

But we need to look at all of that through the context of the conversations we've already had. Those who cause others to suffer for their own gain will certainly lead unfulfilling lives, because fulfillment is found in serving others. And no one in their right mind would call those people men. Evil, monstrous, despicable? Yes. Men? No.

So, if we look at influence, credibility, and authority with the foundational understanding that being a man means something more than simple biological makeup and that the fuel driving us to become men is fulfillment, which is found in service to others, we can begin to see how each of these factors is nothing more than a tool. No one would ever call a hammer evil or unrighteous. But a hammer can be used to crack a hole in a man's skull as easily as it can be used to build a beautiful home.

Consider some of the most evil men throughout history: Adolf Hitler, Heinrich Himmler, Joseph Stalin, Nero, Genghis Khan, Mao Zedong, and countless others. Can anyone deny that these men had influence, credibility, and authority? Of course not. They clearly did.

Now, consider some of the greatest men throughout history: Jesus Christ, George Washington, Theodore Roosevelt, Leonardo da Vinci, Albert Einstein, Gandhi, Martin Luther King Jr., and Abraham Lincoln, to name a few. Can we also not deny that *these* men had influence, credibility, and authority?

What, then, is the difference? It's not the tool but how we wield it that matters.

INFLUENCE

Influence is nothing more than one person's ability to impact another's thoughts or behaviors. *Merriam-Webster* defines influence as "the power to change or affect someone or something; the power to cause changes without directly forcing them to happen."

But notice what's missing from that definition. It does *not* say "negatively" or "positively affect someone or something." In short, influence is amoral. It is neither good nor bad. It simply is. It's up to the wielder of that influence to determine if his or her level of influence leads to positive or negative outcomes.

Now, notice what's present in that definition. Specifically, the phrase, "without directly forcing them to happen." In other words, influence is not taken. Influence is not coerced. Influence is not bribed, blackmailed, bought, or stolen. The *only* way influence is obtained is that it is granted, consciously or unconsciously, by the one who is being influenced.

As I sit here writing these words, I've just wrapped up five hours of brainstorming and discussion with fifteen of my most respected friends. The reason I consider them to be some of my most respected friends is because they have earned it.

As I sat and listened to them talk about some of their most pressing business goals, challenges, and ideas, I found myself scribbling frantically on my notepad, clinging to every word.

The insight they shared with me has the ability to drastically alter the course of my business and the men I work to serve. I acknowledge and honor that. And because I do, I give them my time, attention, and energy, and I act on their recommendations.

Isn't that why we all want influence? Whether you're leading a group of ten thousand or just want your son to make his bed, your level of success is largely determined by the level of influence you have, not *over* those people, but *with* them.

The reality is that you cannot effectively lead people without your ability to influence them.

Now, you may be questioning the previous assertion I made that some of the most horrific men throughout history wielded influence. It's true. They did exhibit levels of influence with *some* people, but certainly not with everyone. With the others, they led through fear, manipulation, coercion, and threats of violence and death.

That isn't influence. And it certainly isn't effective leadership. It's tyranny and dictatorship.

Compliance vs. Commitment

So, what's the problem with tyranny and dictatorship? I think the answer to that question goes without saying, so I'm not going to waste time explaining it. But I do want you to consider that question every time you yell at one of your kids for not doing his or her homework or verbally chastise one of your employees for missing a deadline.

As I ask myself this question, I can't help but feel a tremendous sense of remorse for one of the worst coaching experiences I've ever had or, more accurately, created.

I was coaching my son's Little League baseball team. We were ahead in the last inning. The pitcher had been throwing an incredible game up until that point. He lost it in the ninth, but I had limited depth in my pitching roster, so he had to stay in. As he struggled, I vividly remember yelling at him, "Just throw strikes!" I yelled, berated, and nagged him, believing this would get us the pitches we needed.

It didn't. Things only got worse. A young man who had been so confident in his abilities was now demoralized in front of me, his team, and his family. Truth be told, I can't remember the outcome of that game. In the grand scheme of things, the outcome didn't matter nearly as much as my inappropriate behavior did.

I've thought a lot about that experience since. That was not leadership on my part. That was tyranny. While you might be willing to excuse my behavior as a coach (many of us have been there), and I'm not likely to lead the next genocide simply because I yelled at one of my pitchers in a heated moment, it's similar behavior all the same.

Anger and hostility do not garner influence. Resist the temptation to resort to them at all costs. Lashing out at a player, child, employee, wife, etc., is emotional (more on that later), and it does not foster commitment. It may foster compliance, but certainly not commitment.

Compliance is easy. All anyone needs to foster compliance is something to dangle over those he or she wishes to control—employment, income, threat of violence, imprisonment, etc. In fact, all you really need is to make others think you have something to dangle over them, even if you don't.

I won't lie. Attempting to gain compliance from others is enticing because it requires little effort. If I'm trying to get my children to do the dishes, barking, "Because I said so," when they ask me, "Whyyyyyy?" is significantly easier than sitting them down, looking them in the eye, and explaining to them the inextricable link between prosperity and responsibility.

The same holds true in the workforce. Although subordinates may not whine, "Whyyyyyy?" when tasked with a new project, they may hesitate to ask that question genuinely or to seek clarification from you at all.

They may simply put their heads down and go to work. "What's wrong with that?" you might ask.

The simple answer is that when people comply without committing, their work is likely to be inferior to what they're capable of. And in the case of those you care about—whether they're your children, employees, or anyone else—they won't receive the benefit of learning the significantly more important lesson behind the work, the why and the how.

My friend, performance coach Brett Bartholomew, introduced me to the concept of "Compliance vs. Commitment" in his book, *Conscious Coaching: The Art and Science of Building Buy-In*.[1] Garnering compliance is easy when you're in a position of power and authority. Alternatively, as Brett shares, commitment is what genuine leaders (not tyrants and dictators) are after. A committed individual cares about the cause. A committed individual takes more pride in his work because of it. A committed individual will exercise creativity in his pursuit of easier, more efficient, and more profitable ways of doing things.[2]

When put like that, it's hard to imagine why any boss, manager, father, coach, etc., wouldn't be willing to pursue commitment more often. But given the fact that garnering commitment takes significantly longer than garnering compliance, we can begin to understand why bad leaders are so abundant and good ones seem to be so scarce.

There is one primary difference between compliance and commitment. Whereas compliance is forced, commitment is voluntary. Your influence is what drives people to commit to the cause, whether that's a more connected family or a more profitable company that serves its clients well. And influence is a direct result of authority and credibility.

AUTHORITY

Authority differs from influence in that it is typically derived from a separate, qualified source—not necessarily you alone. For example, your authority to lead your team at work may be granted by your manager or boss or the owner of your company. Your authority to lead your family is granted by God (more on that in a minute). Your authority to sit on a school board or other elected position is granted by your constituents.

Regarding my comment about authority granted by God, you will garner the support of those you wish to lead only if they recognize the authority by which you act. For example, if you believe your authority is derived from God and your wife does not, your influence will only go so far. The same would hold true if I needed surgery and the "doctor" performing it received his degree from a third-rate institution in a Third World country. You can see how that would undermine my confidence in the so-called doctor.

I've often felt the same phenomenon in traditional forms of education. I remember the level of disdain I felt as I entered my first year of college. I received a full academic scholarship (which I lost after a semester of not showing up to class).

I vividly remember sitting in a writing class. I asked our professor, "What books have you written?" to which she replied, "I haven't." She then proceeded to rattle off her credentials and her level of education as if that was supposed to impress me. Needless to say, it didn't. I dropped out of college soon thereafter.

Sure, we can debate whether that was a wise choice, but the point I'm attempting to make is that authority is subjective. It is largely determined by both those who would grant it and those who would recognize the authority by which you act.

Where influence leads down the chain of command, authority leads up it. If you have any hope of leading others effectively, you must learn to lead in both directions.

While your ability to lead comes well before you get any particular title, securing authority is another crucial step in picking up the mantle of leadership and serving those around you.

If you have no authority over others, you will be less likely to garner the commitment necessary to win. Imagine me as a father attempting to get my neighbor's children to do the chores around my house. Or consider how difficult it would be to pull employees from one department to work in mine without the right to do so. Or, in the political realm, what would likely happen if I attempted to pass legislation for a neighboring state?

This is the point where many men get lost. They seem to believe that if they want authority, it must be for their own selfish desires and pursuits at the expense of those they wish to lead. It may be true that the quest for authority can be selfish, but why do we operate so often in false dichotomies? Is it possible to both acknowledge your own desires and have a heart to serve others at the same time?

I believe that it is not only possible, but absolutely necessary. Why do we sit when we should stand? Why do we remain quiet when we should speak up? Why do we cower when we should act?

If your heart is pure and you have the desire to serve others through effective leadership, you should seek authority—not shirk it in fear of what others may think of your ambition.

When I was a young boy, my mom once told me, "Ryan, most people don't like to see others succeed. It threatens them." She often told me stories of her childhood, when she would excel in school only to be mocked by those who didn't. It stung at the time, and she was tempted to "dumb herself down" so as not to put herself in front of the pack. We've all been tempted at times to shrink when we should rise.

I'm reminded of one of my favorite quotes by author Marianne Williamson:

> Our deepest fear is not that we are inadequate. Our deepest fear is that we are powerful beyond measure. It is our light, not our darkness that most frightens us. We ask ourselves, "Who am I to be brilliant, gorgeous, talented, fabulous?" Actually, who are you not to be? You are a child of God. Your playing small does not serve the world. There is nothing enlightened about shrinking so that other people won't feel insecure around you. We are all meant to shine, as children do. We were born to make manifest the glory of God that is within us. It's not just in some of us; it's in everyone. And as we let our own light shine, we unconsciously give other people permission to do the same. As we are liberated from our own fear, our presence automatically liberates others.[3]

The only point I take issue with is that I do not think we are frightened by our light, but frightened by others' perceptions of us when we decide to shine it. But as Williamson said, you *were* born to shine your light, and I believe you were born to lead others well.

Authority alone, however, does not entitle you to the followership of those you wish to lead. It's simply another arrow in the quiver of effective leadership. Considering all that is stacked against us, we should take all the arrows we can get.

CREDIBILITY

If influence is the power to get the commitment of others and authority is the right to do so, credibility is the fuel required to do both.

When I was a financial advisor, I was instructed and constantly reminded to inform my clients that, "Past performance does not guarantee future results" (or a variation of that theme). While the phrase certainly holds true for mutual funds and just about every other investment vehicle out there, it's less true (if not completely wrong) when it comes to the performance of men.

Barring few exceptions, you can be fairly certain that what another individual has produced in the past is likely to be what he produces in the present and future. The exception is the male who is on the path to making himself a man. But as we all are aware, change happens slowly and gradually.

The reality is that you are going to be judged by your track record. If you have a track record of losing, you're likely to be viewed as a loser. I know it's taboo to label people these days. Labels (unless they're affirmative) are often viewed as constraints and thereby rejected. But if you're being honest, you know that not only do you place these "constraints" on yourself, you place them on others too.

The same holds true, however, for winners. Winners win. Losers lose. The reason you might consider that to be a trite comment is because it's absolutely true. Have you ever wondered why Tom Brady continues to prove to be the greatest quarterback of all time? It's because he's a winner. You know it. I know it. Everyone knows it. Regarding credibility, does anyone doubt that Brady has it? Of course not.

What you've done in the past, for better or worse, will largely predict your future. It's not a secret. So to be viewed as credible, you have to build credibility. It's a painstakingly slow process but completely worth the effort.

Start from the Bottom

One question I'm often met with is, "How can I build credibility when I don't have much to start with?" It's very similar to the old chicken-and-egg paradox. While you and I can debate the answer to that question all day long, when it comes to credibility, there's no debate: you must build it from the ground up.

How do you do that? Theodore Roosevelt said, "Do what you can, with what you have, where you are." It's simple, but it's not easy.

In 1998, at the age of seventeen, my mom and stepfather instructed me to get a job. The only thing I'd done up to that point to earn any money was to sweep floors at my stepfather's cabinetry shop and shovel dirt for a landscaper my family knew. They would pay me under the table, and it was enough to buy a new video game or take my high school sweetheart on a date on Saturday night. But this was different.

They wanted me to get a real job. One Saturday, I took the Ford Bronco to a neighboring town much larger than the one of two thousand people where I lived to look for work. After inquiring at over two dozen places where I'd *like* to work, I ended up in Burger King, asking if they were hiring.

Fortunately (or unfortunately, depending on how you look at it), the manager was in. She asked if I had time for an interview on the spot. I did. After a ridiculously short interview with someone who, frankly, held very little influence (Authority? Yes. Influence? No.) with me, I was offered my first real job: Burger King employee. (Side note: After I left that interview, I backed the Bronco into another vehicle and ended up having to use my first few weeks of paychecks to pay for the front grill I broke.)

Needless to say, Burger King was disgusting work. I would come home after a shift caked in what seemed like a two-inch layer of burger grease. The people were rude; my coworkers, insane; and my boss acted more like a prepubescent teenager than the leader of a team of twenty-five.

I quit not long after I started.

I worked various jobs over the next several years, each one an improvement over the previous one. Now, twenty-three years later, I have the most incredible job on the planet: I have conversations with amazingly successful people and inspire men to live the lives they dream of. But I didn't go from line cook at Burger King to interviewing men like Ben Shapiro, Terry Crews, Tim Tebow, Matthew McConaughey, and Ted Nugent overnight. No, it was a process of earning and establishing credibility. By no means am I knocking anyone who works in fast food, but it should be viewed as a temporary stepping-stone to something more.

You are a builder. During the reign of Solomon in 957 BC, an incredible temple unlike anything ever seen before was built. On May 10, 2013, One World Trade Center's final component, the skyscraper's spire, was installed, making it the tallest building in the United States at 1,776 feet. *Homo sapiens* have been on this planet for hundreds of thousands of years, and in that time, we have been building buildings, vehicles, modern inventions, tools, etc. We're hardwired to do it. I would contend that a man who isn't actively building something—his career, his family, his legacy—isn't quite the same as the man who is.

PROVE YOURSELF WORTHY

We live in a society that currently welcomes and honors mediocrity. The "body-positive" movement is one such example. Its proponents would have you accept yourself just the way you are. They're talking about your physical appearance, of course, but they're also advocating that you should just embrace an inferior version of who you could potentially be, both inside and out.

You'll often hear these people say, "Just be yourself." While I can understand the need to feel confident in who you are with all of your oddities, strangeness, and quirks, I'll never believe that "be yourself" means "be less that you're capable of." No, instead, "be yourself" means "be actively working on the ideal version of yourself."

Do you really believe that if you are to establish any sort of influence, authority, and credibility with others, they will accept the fact that you are "being yourself" as collateral?

Imagine walking into a Fortune 500 company to interview as a C-level executive, expecting him to hire you because someone convinced you the path to happiness was to settle, and you believed them.

No, if you want to establish credibility with others, you have to prove you're capable of leading others well. Building credibility is not theoretical. It's practical. Only when you show that you're capable of accomplishing the task at hand will others begin to notice.

You may ask, "Ryan, who are you to tell me I need to prove myself?"

Frankly, it isn't just me who believes this. Every other person on the planet believes it too, whether they'll vocalize it or not. In today's climate, it's more important to *feel* good than it is to *be* good. But feelings only get you so far. When push comes to shove, people will always choose a capable man over an emotional one.

So, where does one start? With a single step. That's it. Sal Frisella, president of 1st Phorm, one of the top nutritional supplement companies in the U.S., says, "Left foot, right foot." Another good friend of mine, exercise equipment manufacturer Sorinex President Bert Sorin, says, "Brick by brick." I echo something similar: Take the next first step.

The path to making a hundred sales calls this week is the first call.

The path to kicking addiction starts with one simple win against temptation.

The path to paying off all your debt is to make one extra payment.

The path to losing fifty pounds is to cut out processed sugars.

The path to salvaging your marriage is to do what you say you'll do.

The path to starting a podcast is to purchase a microphone.

The path to running a marathon is to put your tennis shoes on.

Get it? If you want to build credibility, which is a requirement of leadership, be credible. Start small. Be consistent. Don't fall backward. Before you know it, you'll find people turning to you for guidance, counsel, and direction.

PART II

THE MINDSETS OF MASCULINE LEADERSHIP

*If the highest aim of a captain were to preserve his ship,
he would keep it in port forever.*

—*Thomas Aquinas*

Anything you hope to make a reality must first start in the mind. Therefore, any influence, authority, and credibility you hope to garner with others must first start with yourself.

One topic I often address (because others ask for it so often) is how a man can win back the attention, admiration, and love of his wife. What is almost exclusively true for men who are either going through a marital separation or dealing with a looming divorce is that they have an insatiable fixation on dealing with the external factors (lack of intimacy, resentment, and even hostility toward one another) of the relationship without a willingness to deal with the internal factors of themselves (anger, commitment issues, lack of confidence, etc.).

I know that certainly holds true with me. My wife and I were separated for a time in 2008, and I was absolutely convinced that once she changed, our marriage would resume and become what we had both envisioned when we committed to each other four years earlier. To my frustration, that didn't work. It wasn't until I learned that if I hope to fix the outside world around me, I must first fix the internal world within me, that we began to reconcile.

Unironically, it's the internal factors (those within your control) that predominantly determine your external reality.

But I understand our desire to fix the external before the internal. It's much easier to assume that once the world around you changes, your perception of it will as well. While that may be true to a degree, it is much more effective and efficient to change yourself first and allow the outside world to adapt to you (that's the subject of my first book, *Sovereignty: The Battle for the Hearts and Minds of Men*).

HAVE, DO, BE vs. BE, DO, HAVE

There is a common misconception among many that in order to achieve what you desire, you must first have what is required. This is backward thinking. For example, many people believe that if they have money, they can do the things they've dreamed of, and that will make them happy. It isn't true. I know plenty of wealthy people who are miserable. Conversely, I know plenty of broke people who are happy.

I'm often reminded of men like Robin Williams, Anthony Bourdain, Ernest Hemingway, and Junior Seau, who by any objective measure had so much to be grateful for—but they all killed themselves. I have no idea what demons they were dealing with; I only bring it up to make the point that external factors do not paint the entire picture. There is something much deeper going on here.

Occasionally, even I catch myself feeling down, depressed, and in despair, though I have an incredible life. I can't fully explain it. In those moments of darkness, I objectively know that I shouldn't feel this way, but it doesn't seem to help.

So, can we honestly say that our external factors determine how we feel about ourselves? At best, externalities can give us a temporary high or relieve us from our chronic pain. But it's a fleeting reprieve. And it's fickle, often replaced by the next great high or low we experience.

Instead, I suggest that we flip the notion of *Have, Do, Be* on its head, and embrace the *Be, Do, Have* mindset. If you can learn to be fulfilled first, you will do the things you want to do and will inevitably have all that you desire.

It all starts with the mind. Can the man who picks up other people's trash for a living really be fulfilled? Can the man who works as a janitor at his local high school find purpose in his work? Can the man who is miserable with the work he performs discover meaning in the misery? He can . . . if he chooses to.

WHERE YOUR MIND GOES, RESULTS WILL FOLLOW

Look, I get it, this is a dark conversation. It's especially dark for those who feel as if they've hit rock bottom, with no visible way out. Couple that with feeling that you're literally incapable of changing your own environment, and it becomes a desperate situation.

But have hope. I come with good news. The good news is that you aren't obligated to follow the *Have, Do, Be* model. You can, if you decide to, follow the *Be, Do, Have* model. It's a choice. And it's a choice I encourage you to make right now.

The first path leads to a place of inadequacy, where you're reliant on the people and experiences around you to determine your fulfillment. The latter path is where you grab your life by the balls and make of it what you will. And, subsequently, lead others to do the same.

Worded that way, I'm not sure it's much of a choice. What remains is only how we're going to do it, and then get to work making it a reality.

So, we're going to start where any great battle starts: with an idea, a concept. More precisely, we're going to start with your mindset for masculine leadership and begin to articulate some basic concepts you must internalize before you garner influence, authority, and credibility with others:

- Overcome the Ease of Modernity
- Don't Be a Superhero
- Lead before the Title
- Render Yourself Obsolete

Don't feel discouraged as we work though these Mindsets of Masculine Leadership. It's easy for us to fall into the trap of imposter syndrome. I did!

When I started my podcast over seven years ago, I was a know-nothing nobody. As I lay in my bed in those early years, trying to get any amount of sleep I could, I would often find myself conflicted in my desires and who I believed myself to be at the time.

I would often beat myself up as a fake, a phony, and tell myself that I had no business discussing masculinity and manliness when I felt so inferior as a man myself. In short, I felt like a fraud. And maybe, to a degree, that was true seven years ago. It isn't now—but only because I embraced in my mind who I was and, more importantly, who I had the potential to become.

CHAPTER FOUR

OVERCOME THE EASE OF MODERNITY

*Do not pray for easy lives. Pray to be stronger men. Do
not pray for tasks equal to your powers. Pray for powers
equal to your tasks. Then the doing of the work shall be
no miracle, but you shall be the miracle.*

—*Phillips Brooks*

Two days ago, I thought I was having a truly bad day. I started by
missing my alarm (yes, it happens from time to time), and it all went
downhill from there.

My family and I had just returned from a week-long vacation in
Mexico, and while the time away was nice, I found it difficult to rest and
relax, knowing how much work I was falling behind on.

When we leave as a family for vacation, our merchandise shipping
at Order of Man shuts down because my son runs the store. The day we
got back, we were met with more than three hundred orders to fill. All
well and good—except the store computer was acting up and making it
damn near impossible to fill any orders with any amount of efficiency.
And knowing Christmas was coming up and people had ordered gifts
from us made it all the more stressful.

In the wake of fighting with my computer for hours, I decided to go
to the store and buy a new one. I spent a bit over $700 and walked out
twenty minutes later with a new computer. It took me an hour to get it
up and running, find all my passwords, create new ones for the ones I'd
forgotten, and finally get logged in to the back end of our store.

By the time we were again ready to ship orders, it was late afternoon, and we had shipped less than 5 percent of them.

That night when I finally put my head on my pillow, I thought about how horrible the day had been. Then it hit me: It really wasn't that bad of a day. Considering all that other people might be going through in that moment, I felt like a bit of a tool for complaining about what, in all likelihood, would one day be a funny memory.

Think about that scenario with me for a minute. My alarm on my phone went off in the morning, which meant I had electricity. It also meant I own a freaking supercomputer so small it fits in my pocket. Thirty minutes or so later, I rolled out of bed. It's cold this time of year in Maine, so I walked over to the wall to turn the temperature in my house from sixty-five degrees to seventy degrees. (Higher than any real man should set his thermostat. Don't judge me.) Then I put on my clothes. I don't own sheep or a cotton field, so I didn't make the clothes. I don't know how to sew, so I didn't stitch the fabric together to make the garments; I just put them on without a second thought. I went downstairs and grabbed a banana. Not a banana I grew; not a banana I picked. I just grabbed one off the counter and ate it. Then I threw the peel in the garbage, which will be picked up for me and taken to who knows where.

Next, I went down to the store and saw the three hundred–plus orders. I griped about it, but, in that moment, I didn't consider that those orders represented income for me to put food on my family's table and a roof over our head. It also meant that hundreds of people believe in what we're doing enough to spend their hard-earned money at our store.

On the subject of money, no one gave me any bills, no gold coins were exchanged, and no physical transaction took place. It all happened somewhat mysteriously in the ethernet while I was traveling in a country more than 3,750 miles away, but which took my family only four hours to reach.

When my modern feat of incredible engineering (the laptop we use) wasn't working as quickly as I liked, I drove five miles up the road in my 2015 GMC Sierra to buy a new one. The store had hundreds of them in stock. I was actually frustrated with how many options there were. Do you hear that? I was frustrated by the abundance. (I'm insane.)

It took me an hour to get our store running. When those sixty minutes were over, I was immediately connected to millions of people I'll never meet or see.

Later that night, I put my head on my pillow—a pillow I personally picked, as it has just the right amount of volume, on the bed I personally picked out as it has just the right amount of firmness.

I said goodnight to my wife—the beautiful woman who lay comfortably in my bed as she trusted me fully to lead our family well—rolled over, and went to sleep.

What an asshole I am.

Frankly, what assholes most of us are. What many of us believe to be problems aren't really problems at all.

But that's what the ease of modernity does to us. It messes with our perception of discomfort. Because it messes with that perception, it drives us to make mountains out of molehills. And that keeps us and those we wish to lead from dreaming big and aligning our action and commitment with those dreams.

Conversely, knowing real suffering and emerging from it gives us the confidence needed to achieve our greatest desires and help others do the same. If you have dealt with death, disease, bankruptcy, famine, poverty, or tyranny, can any mere inconveniences be all that challenging for you?

COMFORT MAKES YOU COMPLACENT

I'm a man who enjoys the comfort and ease of modernity. I really am. I like nice things. I like a beautiful home. I like to be dressed well. I like to buy stuff. I like to be warm when I wake up. I like having internet service. I really enjoy all these things and more. But while there is a place and time to enjoy what we have and the fruits of our labor, there is a place and time to put it all away and do something hard.

Because life is hard. Or at least it can be. It *will* be. You're going to be met with the inevitable suffering this world has to offer, and if you aren't capable of discerning what is hard and what isn't, you're going to crumble. There is only one way to harden yourself for what is to come: you have to get out ahead of it.

I've seen grown men fall apart completely at the slightest suffering, and while I try not to judge any man whose actions do not impact me or mine, it's pretty telling to watch someone turn into a sniveling little boy when pressed.

The truth is that comfort makes you complacent. Complacency leads to unnecessary hardship. When you're on top of your game, it's easy to believe nothing can or will happen. But when it does, you'll find yourself incapable of weathering the storm—hardly a redeeming quality for a man who wishes to lead.

So why do we wait until the situation is dire to change, to become stronger, to fix ourselves?

First, I'd suggest that we're blinded, or at least distracted, by comfort.

There's a game my two oldest boys (who are fourteen and eleven) like to play. They like to sneak up behind me and attempt to rear naked choke me (a common submission in Brazilian Jiu-Jitsu, in which your opponent wraps his arms around your neck from behind, limiting the supply of blood to your brain and causing you to pass out) while my guard is down. It typically happens while I'm lying on the couch, watching a show, or in deep conversation with my wife or a friend. The entire point of the game is to get the better of me while I'm distracted. (They've only gotten me a few times.)

While my sons laugh and joke at their attempts to best their old man, it's a great analogy for what happens in real life. Just as we let our guard down, something sneaks up and attempts to strangle us. The car's transmission goes out. One of our children breaks an arm. We lose our job. We or someone we love is met with a health scare. Or all of the above.

The other reason we wait so long to steel ourselves against life's woes is that doing so requires effort. Most of us choose the path of least resistance when what we should be doing is choosing the path of most resistance.

Look, I'm not suggesting we need to make life hard on ourselves for the sake of it being hard. There must be purpose to the suffering. I'm not asking you to become a masochist. I'm asking you to consider that volunteering to be uncomfortable will likely serve you and those you wish to lead well down the road.

Be careful in letting down your guard. You don't need to be a paranoid psycho, either. Just be vigilant (more on that later). We know that the storm is coming. We don't know when or where, but it is coming. Ready or not, it will arrive.

REACT OR RESPOND—THE CHOICE IS YOURS

I've spent most of my life in relatively moderate climates. I lived in Southern California as a kid, until my family moved to a small town in southern Utah when I was thirteen. It snowed in the winter but not much, and it didn't stick around for long. After high school, I moved further south to St. George, Utah, where the coldest it gets in the dead of winter is the low thirties. Needless to say, I was not accustomed to or comfortable with cold weather.

That all changed in 2019, when my wife, four children, two dogs, and I moved to central Maine, where it's not uncommon for the temperatures in the winter to get to the single digits and even dip into the negatives.

Fortunately, when I moved here, I was smart enough to ask the locals what we needed to do to get ready for the winter. They suggested a snowplow, multiple heat sources, and a generator hooked into the electrical panel of our home. I took care of all three immediately.

I also learned there was a common phrase people here live by: "You're either preparing for or dealing with winter." Wasn't that the truth! Between chopping wood, securing provisions, growing a garden, and preserving food, our springs and summers have become preparatory seasons for what we know will inevitably come.

The same holds true for the rest of our lives: "You're either preparing for or dealing with _____." Or, at least, you *should* be. If you aren't, you're going to find yourself in a difficult situation when presented with a serious challenge.

Regardless of what that challenge is, you're going to have to deal with it, right? The only difference is whether you'll react or respond.

Reacting to a situation is typically done in the short term, without much thought or planning. If a car cuts you off as you're barreling down the road at sixty-five miles an hour, you have a split second to react and keep yourself from plowing into the vehicle in front of you. There is a time and place for reaction. In the example I just provided, not reacting to being cut off only results in destruction and death.

But the problem with reacting is that it isn't always well thought out and, given the limited information and time we have with which to make a decision in these moments, we may find ourselves choosing incorrectly, putting ourselves and others at risk.

Responding, on the other hand, is more about making calculated decisions only after you've considered and weighed the options. Responding gives you more time to think clearly about the scenarios you may be presented with and gives you the capacity to make decisions logically and rationally versus erratically and emotionally.

Consider the scenario of a car pulling out in front of you. If you're a responsive individual, you may consider that you're coming up to a particularly dangerous crossroad. You might choose to scan your surroundings as you go through intersections. You might choose to slow down, knowing that a car may pull out in front of you. You might avoid certain roads altogether during particularly busy times of the day. There is an infinite number of choices you can make, knowing that danger might present itself.

The point I'm making regarding responsiveness is that you're getting out ahead of a potential threat. So how does the react/respond conversation relate to overcoming the ease of modernity?

Very simply. Are you going to wait for life to get hard before you do something about it? Are you going to wait until you're presented with a difficult scenario before doing the work required to navigate it? Are you going to wait for a catastrophic moment in time to improve yourself? I hope not.

Think about how many men start working out and eating better only *after* they've been diagnosed with a medical condition. Consider how many men wait to build their network only after they've been laid off. Or how many men work to improve their relationship with their wife only after she suggests a separation or divorce.

A responsive man is one who has embraced overcoming the ease of modernity. A responsive man knows life is going to be hard, whether he wants it to be or not. A responsive man is willing to do the work—exercise, diet, train, study, write, journal, reflect, network, grind, etc.—*now*, knowing that winter is coming. And gentlemen, it *is* coming.

Are you going to do the hard work now or the hard work later? If you do it now, life will get easier. If you put it off until later, it will be harder than it needs to be.

MANUFACTURING HARDSHIP

So, with all of that said, and in the absence of hardship in modern society, you need to learn to manufacture it. And not only for yourself. As an aspiring or current leader in your family, business, and community, it's your job to manufacture hardship for yourself and those you care about. Remember, this isn't all about you. The entire point of leadership is to serve others and assist them in becoming more capable, proficient, fulfilled humans themselves.

To manufacture hardship, I've found it best to break it down into four realms: physical, mental, emotional, and spiritual.

Physical

I've found the physical realm to be the easiest for most men to operate in. There is no confusion or guesswork about "embracing the suck" that comes with pushing your body to its fullest capacity.

The real question is what, specifically, you are going to do. With all the options—strength training, powerlifting, high intensity interval training (HIIT), CrossFit, boxing, Jiu-Jitsu, long-distance running, cycling, swimming, etc.—it can be difficult to know where to start. In a perfect world, you'd be able to do them all. As you know, we don't live in a perfect world, and you can't. You don't have time for it all.

I recommend that you pick the one (or two) that A) most appeals to you and B) can keep you engaged for the longest period of time. CrossFit and Jiu-Jitsu are what do it for me. Yeah, I know, "CrossFit doesn't work," and "There are better forms of martial arts for self-defense" than Jiu-Jitsu. Maybe that's true; maybe it isn't. That's not the point. The point is to be in the game indefinitely. If you try to convince me I should be a runner, but I'm not interested in running, I'm not going to do it for very long, if at all.

The same holds true for those under your care. I used to be convinced that the greatest thing I could do for my children was push them in the direction I was going. That didn't work. They quickly lost interest and reverted to old patterns and habits. Just as you have activities and interests that appeal to you, so do they.

About a year ago, one of my sons said to me, "Dad, I like power-lifting more than Jiu-Jitsu." It stung a bit because we trained so often together. But in the end, it's about his growth, not mine. And if power-lifting is his thing, so be it. As long as my kids are doing something physical, I'm all about it.

Mental

Manufacturing mental hardship is imperative in this day and age. As with any of the four realms we're addressing, your mental fortitude is subjective, as is your interpretation of the events around you.

This is why you'll often see two men respond very differently to similar situations. While one of these men may view his circumstances as the worst thing in the world, the other may choose to see them as a tremendous opportunity for growth and expansion.

The greatest difference between the two is their level of mental fortitude. The great news is that, like physical strength, mental strength can be built.

So where do you start to build your mental fortitude? I suggest that the best place to start is exactly where you don't want to. We all have things on our list we don't want to do but know they need to get done. Do those things first.

Early in my financial planning career, I was tasked to make a list of potential prospects. These were people I knew—relatives, acquaintances, neighbors, friends, etc. I made a "prospect list" of about two hundred people. On this list were people I had no problem calling, but roughly 10 percent were people I wouldn't want to call. I named it my "chicken list."

Naturally, I put off calling these people till the very end. When I finally exhausted the rest of my list and worked up the courage to call the ones on my chicken list, I was surprised how easy it was. Many of the people on that portion of the list were happy to meet with me, and a few of them wished I would have called earlier, as they had just started working with a new financial planner. Damn! Why did I wait so long?

To build mental fortitude, you're going to have to move your chicken list to the front of your task stack.

- Ask that woman you've been eyeing out on a date.
- Have that difficult conversation with your son or daughter.
- Ask your wife about your performance as a husband.
- Ask for a promotion.
- Call a potential new client.
- Say yes to something you would normally say no to.
- Say no to something you would normally say yes to.
- Hit "publish" on the podcast you recorded three months ago.
- Write the first word of the book you've been dreaming about for years.

The first step is alwayss the hardest when it comes to building mental fortitude. That's why you need to get it out of the way and just start. A word of caution: DO NOT attach unnecessary meaning to the outcome of your actions. Sure, analyze the outcome to see if you can improve, but if you measure your willingness to start against the likelihood of the desired outcome, you're going to be sadly disappointed. In fact, that's a huge part of mental fortitude—doing the work in spite of how you feel about it or whether the desired outcome is guaranteed.

Emotional

Here's what you need to know: contrary to popular belief (perpetuated in the self-help space), emotions are your friend.

You wouldn't experience them if they weren't meant to serve you in some way. We're going to talk a lot about this in Chapter Eleven, "Aggression," so, for now, I just need you to trust me on this. Your emotions can help you if you allow them to. If you don't allow them to help you, they won't magically disappear. In fact, they'll become your worst enemy.

See, we're often led to believe that our so-called "negative" emotions should be driven away. Because it's impossible to drive away your emotions, you're left with only one option: stop the thing that's making you emotional in the first place.

Wrong answer. If you run at the slightest sign of emotional hardship, you'll never do anything worthwhile or meaningful. Next time you feel your emotions welling up, I challenge you not to run from them. That isn't strength; it's weakness.

Instead, stop, temporarily disengage from the situation you find yourself in, evaluate what you're feeling and why, then reengage in the activity with a new and healthy perspective. Emotional resilience is found in confronting your emotions, not hiding from them.

Spiritual

I'm amazed how often I hear from men who believe that being spiritual makes you either weak or subservient to a higher power. It doesn't. It simply means you're aware of another realm that can serve you and the people you care about.

I wish that everything we experienced was tangible—that you could recognize it all with the five senses. It would certainly be easier to understand if that were the case. Unfortunately, you can't. Your spirituality requires faith—faith in the unknown, faith in the unseen, and faith in the unprovable.

But developing faith seems to be difficult for many men. How can a man be expected to believe in something he cannot see? By listening. Not from his ears but from his soul. When a man learns to listen to the Holy Spirit, he taps into something much deeper than himself and sets himself on a path to meaning and fulfillment—not *in spite* of the suffering, but *because* of it. However spirituality manifests itself to you, your spiritual strength is found and developed by listening and acting on it.

Years ago, my wife and I were looking to purchase a new home. On one of our drives around town, we came across a house that had potential. We pulled into the driveway and called our real estate agent. He was not able to meet us at the time, so we decided to get out of the car and simply walk around the property. I noticed that the back sliding door was unlocked, so I opened it and stepped inside the vacant home. As my wife and I entered the house, we both felt an overwhelming sense of evil. We looked at each other and knew instantly we were feeling the same thing. We left immediately and drove off.

Later, we found out that a squatter was living in that old, abandoned house. I'm not sure what would have happened if we'd kept looking—maybe nothing—but I wasn't willing to find out.

Let me reiterate: the way to develop spiritual strength is to listen for it and act on it. You'll never fully understand why you feel the way you do in certain situations, and that's okay. It's your job as a man to tap into and utilize *all* the tools at your disposal.

WRAP UP

I think we can all acknowledge that, in the grand scheme of things, modern life is pretty easy.

No one really expects much of anyone; there are very few consequences for underperformance; everyone seems to be fixated more on their own and others' feelings than on thriving, winning, and excelling on all fronts.

According to Greek mythology, the gods became so bored in their state of perfection that in order to pass time and entertain themselves, they decided to create and populate the earth with creatures of all kinds, including humans.

What fascinates me is that the gods had become so bored in their state of perpetual bliss that they needed something—anything—with which to occupy themselves.

I can't help but think that in a way, we have become the gods. We have created an environment that contains very few threats to our existence. While I appreciate the luxuries of modernity, we too have become bored, complacent, and sedated.

So what do we do? We make up dumb shit to worry about to pass the time. We argue about pronouns and Dr. Seuss books. We create drama. We bicker among ourselves and mock others purely for entertainment. We make mountains out of molehills and relish in manipulating others for our personal gain.

The truth is that we're bored, and too few of us have attached meaning, purpose, and significance to the pain and suffering that come with pursuing something truly and intrinsically valuable.

We run from pain, inoculate ourselves against it, and then wonder why there is no deep satisfaction in our lives.

I would submit to you that maybe the absence of pain and suffering is not the end state to aim for (lest we become bored like the Greek gods), but that strife, struggle, and toil shouldered in a meaningful pursuit are what keep us sane and fulfilled.

Consider that maybe the reason you are unhappy is because the world around you is so great, and you have no challenge to push against. Also consider what meaningful pain you would be willing to endure if it meant a life of fulfillment. Then, get to work in all ways of making yourself capable of bearing it.

RULES FOR OVERCOMING THE EASE OF MODERNITY

1. **Embrace Discomfort.** Consider that the ease of modernity is making you soft and pathetic. This does not exactly make a great foundation for building influence and authority. Identify all the ways you've made life easier for yourself, and work to systematically remove the creature comforts from your life—even if just periodically. Take cold showers, walk to work, have the difficult conversation, ask for a raise, and be a man who can become comfortable with discomfort.

2. **Respond to Your Circumstances.** Men get out ahead of potential problems and situations. Don't wait until your circumstances become a problem to address them. Anticipate what could possibly go wrong and formulate a plan now, before it's too late. That's the difference between responding and reacting.

3. **Manufacture Hardship.** Life is going to be hard sometimes. You can either deal with hardship when it arises, or you can make yourself more capable of dealing with it when it does. The Greek poet Archilochus said, "We do not rise to the level of our expectations, we fall to the level of our training." Train hard (and expect others to) when you *don't* have to, and you'll be more capable of dealing with life when it tries to kick you in the teeth.

CHAPTER FIVE

DON'T BE A SUPERHERO

*The urge to save humanity is almost always a false front
for the urge to rule.*

—H. L. Mencken

In the summer of 2018, my mother called me and said, "Ryan, your dad is in the hospital. He had a heart attack."

This wasn't the first time I had received such a call. A few years earlier, she had delivered the same news. He recovered fairly quickly then, and I thought this time would be no different. So I brushed it off.

A few days later, my mom called me again. "Ryan, your dad isn't doing well. He's not recovering from the heart attack as he should, and his internal organs are struggling." I brushed it off again.

Another couple of days passed before I received another call. "Ryan, your dad is likely not going to make it. You need to come see him and say goodbye." I reluctantly packed my bags and headed to California.

I lived in Utah, and I made the trip as quickly as I could. About thirty minutes from the hospital, I received another call from my mom. "Ry, where are you!" I heard something different in her voice that time, but I wrote it off to the stress of the situation.

"I'm about thirty minutes away. I'll be there as quickly as I can."

When I arrived at the hospital, she greeted me with tears in her eyes. "Where is Dad?" I asked.

"Ry," she said sadly, "he died half an hour ago."

I didn't even get to say goodbye.

I went into his hospital room to see him one last time. Truth be told, I don't really remember much of that visit, except that he lay cold and lifeless on that hospital bed. It was all a bit of a haze.

I loved my dad. Though we'd had a strained relationship for much of my life, he had some amazing redeeming qualities. He was an incredibly hard worker. He knew how to make people laugh. He could make friends like no one I've ever seen. He was one of the most creative and talented men I have ever known.

But in spite of all that, I held quite a bit of resentment toward him. As a young man, I often felt abandoned and neglected by him. He and my mom split when I was three, and although I remember some incredible times we had building LEGOs®, racing Matchbox cars and Micro Machines, and playing G.I. Joe, my bitterness toward him only grew over the years.

It wasn't until I saw him for the last time in that sterile hospital room that I fully forgave him for his perceived transgressions against me. I guess I had always held him to a higher standard than I was willing to hold myself. I realized that day, for everything I felt he did to me that was wrong, I'd returned the favor. For the first time in my life, I no longer saw him as my father, the superhero who failed to live up to my unfair expectations, but as a man (like myself) full of both strengths and weaknesses, virtues and vices.

That day, I decided to take my dad off the pedestal I had wrongly placed him on. It was a hard decision to make. A father is supposed to be there for his boy. A father is supposed to protect and provide for his son. A father is supposed to do everything his child needs—physically, mentally, and emotionally. While I still agree with that sentiment, I knew that I had personally failed in so many similar ways with my own children. How could I, in fairness, excuse my own shortcomings but not my father's?

I see my dad in a different light now. I hope that he and I will see each other again one day, with a new perspective of who the other is as a man. I'm grateful that in his last moments, he taught me that men don't belong on pedestals—not our fathers, and certainly not ourselves.

THE PEDESTALS WE DON'T BELONG ON

But isn't that what we do—place ourselves on pedestals? We walk around like our shit don't stink. We pretend we have things figured out when we really don't. We work tirelessly to impress people we don't even know with skills and talents we don't even have. We let our ego get in the way of our progress and the progress of others.

In short, we put ourselves above others. We believe that not only do we know what's best for us, but we also know what's best for them. If you haven't already figured it out, I've got news for you: you don't, and neither do I.

I know this might sound interesting coming from a man who has not only made a living but started an incredibly powerful movement by teaching other men about masculinity and what it means to be a man. But here's the distinction: I've never once said I have this masculinity thing figured out. I've never once presented myself as the epitome of manliness. I'm on the journey, same as you.

Now, I may know a bit more about a particular subject than you (podcasting, for example), but there are plenty of scenarios, skills, and situations that you know more about than I do.

Leadership has never been about putting yourself above others. In front of others? Possibly. Above others? Never. Pedestals and leadership don't mix.

This is why so many men in positions of authority fall into the trap of "imposter syndrome." I know. I've been there. I've been tasked with a job, assignment, or project that I felt completely unqualified for. To make matters worse, I've attempted to fool not only myself in those situations, but those I could otherwise lead.

Do we honestly believe that by pretending, we won't be figured out? Of course we'll be outed. We aren't fooling anyone when we attempt to pull the wool over their eyes.

Instead, I suggest you step down off the pedestal you have falsely ascended to and own the fact that you don't know everything and you don't have it all figured out. Your job as a leader is not to do everything, but to ensure everything gets done. I know this may sound counterintuitive, but consider the last arrogant boss you had who thought he or she knew everything. Were you more or less influenced by his or her smoke and mirrors? Less, obviously.

You don't have to succumb to imposter syndrome. If you feel like you're an imposter, perhaps it's because you are. Maybe you *are* a fraud. Maybe you *are* a phony. The first step is to tell the truth. You aren't as good as you think you are. And that's okay. You can't lead if you can't or won't see the blind spots that exist. Everyone under your care—your wife, children, neighbors, colleagues, coworkers, team members, etc.—already knows what those blind spots are. Do you?

WHITE KNIGHT

The best definition I've ever heard of leadership is being capable of taking people to a place they could not have imagined going on their own. That's true, but there's a caveat—the people you wish to lead have to *want* to go to that place.

All too often, and due to our own arrogance, we tend to believe that we have the power to rescue everyone. We don't. Have you ever tried to share an opinion, perspective, or insight, only to have the person you're trying to serve scoff at you?

That's the thing about influence: other people have a say in the matter.

I remember a young advisor who had just started working for our financial planning firm. I saw so much potential in that young man, and I could not wait to share everything I knew with him and to see him thrive.

He started hot in the business. He was making plenty of sales calls, securing new clients, and closing deals. Right out of the gate, he was one of the most successful advisors in our office. Then, something changed. Gradually, his winning streak came to a halt. He ran out of clients. He had closed all the business he could. And he struggled from that point to get anywhere.

I'm not really sure why things changed for him. Maybe he lost interest. Maybe he exhausted his list, or his reputation and credibility. Regardless, he came to me one day, asking for advice.

I was flattered. It felt good to be acknowledged, and I knew that if I could take this young advisor and download everything I knew about the business to him, we both would be tremendously successful. I started going to the office early and staying late to mentor him. But while I was initially ecstatic about helping him, that too gradually changed.

Early one morning, he asked me a question about securing referrals from existing clients. Referrals are the lifeblood of any financial advisor, so I was glad he was asking the right question. Unfortunately, every time I offered insight or a suggestion, I was met with, "Yeah, I already tried that." Or, "That doesn't work. What other suggestions do you have?" I finally got so sick of his retorts, I scolded him: "Look, you're wrong! What I'm sharing with you works because it's exactly what I'm doing. If it doesn't work for you, it's because you're doing it wrong or you're lying. Which one is it?"

The mentor/mentee relationship eroded from that moment, and that young man eventually left the business. For weeks, I replayed the relationship in my mind. I'd had such high hopes for him. I recognized how much potential he had. And I wanted him to win. But apparently what he wanted had become at odds with what I wanted for him.

The more I thought about it, the more I realized that I never stopped to ask what he was after. I never stopped to question why he was struggling. I never thought to ask about his personal goals and desires. I never questioned why what I was teaching him wasn't sticking.

As I contemplated about what transpired between us, I began to realize that my personal objective wasn't about him winning at all. It was about *me* winning. I had gotten to the point where I cared more about the success of his business than he did. His success or lack thereof had become more of a referendum on me than him. That's why I was willing to bang my head against the wall over and over to see him win. If he won, I looked good. Period. End of story.

And that's what the White Knight is after. He's after the recognition, the accolades, and the notoriety that come with rescuing others. The White Knight doesn't care about others; he cares about himself. I didn't really care about that young man's success more than I cared about the attention from others I'd receive for helping him achieve it.

How do you know if you truly care about others' winning or if you're in it for your own glory? Very simple. Ask yourself if you would applaud the other party's success even if you had nothing to do with it. If no one ever knew or saw you help, serve, or rescue the other person, would you do it? I hope we'd all say yes in a dire or dangerous situation, but things get cloudy in more nuanced environments like mentoring a student, sharing a strategy with a budding entrepreneur, or working together on a project.

Recognition is a powerful drug. But it's an inferior motive for influence, authority, and credibility. It's fleeting. It's fickle. And it relies solely on factors outside your control: other people who have their own pursuits and desires, and whether people see your performance.

But there is another problem with the White Knight. Consider the term, *White* Knight. We may believe he's called that because he's pure. I don't think he's as pure as we'd immediately like to believe; rather, he is unwilling to get himself dirty. The White Knight is willing to do the work only when it's easy and convenient. The minute the situation gets dangerous, the White Knight bows out. If the White Knight were willing to get into the thick of things when they're at their hardest, he wouldn't be white for very long.

Leadership is a dirty, risky, and often thankless endeavor. But a true leader is willing to get into the dirt and mud. Not because he's confident that he will always emerge victorious, but because the pursuit of serving and leading others is worth the fight. And it is a fight.

Consider one of the most recognizable superheroes we know, Superman. Is he really a hero? He's an alien who can't be hurt. It's easy to rescue others when there is no risk to yourself. That isn't special. That isn't selfless. That isn't worth praise or admiration.

Alternatively, consider another superhero we all know, Batman. Batman is human. Yeah, he's rich, so he's got access to tools, technology, and intel not available to the common man, but he can be hurt. He's mortal.

So, which of the two is more heroic: Superman, who can't be hurt (I know, I know: Kryptonite), or Batman, who can? Who are you more like: Superman (White Knight) or Batman (Dark Knight)?

Every night, Batman goes out at his own personal risk and fights for the innocent against evil. He needs no recognition. His motive is pure. He wants to serve regardless of the praise or recognition he may get and without regard for his own personal safety.

Sure, people praise Superman—but men want to be like Batman.

In fact, the reason we like Batman is the same reason one of the only acceptable moments for a man to cry is while he watches the 1993 film *Rudy* (the other is the birth of his child). It's also the reason the 1980 U.S. Men's Hockey Team story will go down as one of the greatest sporting moments in history. We love the underdog—the man (or team) who's not supposed to emerge victorious but does, not because he's flawless, but because he kicks and claws and fights to win.

LIGHTHOUSE vs. TUGBOAT

Let's talk about the proper role of leadership. Once you know where you're supposed to stand, it becomes much easier to garner influence, credibility, and authority with those you wish to lead and serve.

Most people believe, counterproductively, that the best place to serve people is right where the action is. While I agree that you have to be familiar with and close to those you wish to serve, it's a mistake to get sucked into all that comes with being in the thick of things with those you'd like to lead: the drama, the excuses, the entitlement, the bullshit. It's exhausting and ineffective. Yet, that's what most people do. They dive into the nonsense, hoping they can impact those under their care. But all they end up doing is getting dragged into the noise, fighting and scrapping, and tarnishing themselves along the way.

Don't get me wrong, there is a time and a place for someone to jump into the deep end to save another. But that is the exception, not the rule. Unless there is imminent danger to others, the best place to stand when it comes to leading and serving is a stable and elevated position (not placing yourself on a pedestal, but in a position where you're able to see the entire battlefield more clearly). Not only can you think more clearly from this position, but you're also on stronger ground, which enables you to lift others to safety more efficiently.

That's part of the reason I struggled so much with the aspiring financial advisor I mentioned earlier. I was willing to do the work (with some self-serving motives), but he wasn't. With everything I did and shared, he kicked and thrashed along the way. Not only could I not save him, but I realized that I was underserving my clients, falling behind on other pressing obligations, and wearing myself out (which kept me from serving others well). You can't save anyone who isn't willing to participate in the rescue. If you try, you're likely to drown along with them.

In 2019, my wife and I moved our family to Maine. If you're not familiar with it, Maine has some of the most amazing lighthouses (something southern Utah doesn't have a whole lot of) on the East Coast. One of the first things we did when we arrived was to take our family to see a few of them.

The first lighthouse we visited was the Portland Head Light. Completed in 1791, it is the oldest lighthouse in Maine, and it's beautiful. The original tower measured seventy-two feet and was lit with sixteen whale oil lamps. It's an incredibly impressive sight, and its function is something I think we can all relate to on a personal level.

The function of a lighthouse is to stand tall and resolute, warning incoming vessels of impending danger. If the lighthouse performs correctly, the captain of an arriving ship will avoid the rocky coastline and make it safely to port. If the lighthouse performs incorrectly (or the captain does), the ship is likely to smash against the rocks, sending the cargo and/or the souls aboard to a watery grave.

Contrast the lighthouse with a tugboat. Both serve similar functions—to bring ships safely to shore. Unlike the lighthouse, the tugboat goes out into the water and attaches itself to the ship to pull her in safely.

I watched a tugboat last year work to get a ship into port. It was a painstakingly slow process. She worked for what felt like hours, pulling, pushing, maneuvering, and manipulating a much larger ship through the docks and safely into her resting place.

Like the lighthouse, if the tugboat does its job, the ship she's serving arrives safely. If not, catastrophe.

What's the difference then? Where the lighthouse shines, the tugboat pulls. Where the lighthouse can serve many at once, the tugboat has to focus all her resources on one. Where the lighthouse has an elevated, 360-degree view of danger, the tugboat relies on her memory. Where the lighthouse relies on a vessel's serving herself, the tugboat works tirelessly to move a boat that simply *cannot* do it on her own.

The lighthouse is a proper leader with the proper grounding. The tugboat, while valuable and useful, must manipulate her target to achieve the desired outcome.

The same holds true for you. You cannot leave your post to manipulate others. If you do, consider how many others will be inadequately served in your absence. Your job as a leader is to shine. Period. It's to stand strong and bright as an example of what could potentially be.

That isn't to say you are without flaws. The lighthouse needs to be managed. It needs to be painted. The bulb needs to be replaced. It requires constant maintenance—as do you.

LET PEOPLE FAIL

What if I told you that leadership isn't at all about rescuing other people from their problems but giving them opportunities to fail in controlled environments?

Make no mistake, I'm not talking about setting your people up for failure (that would do anything but garner influence, authority, and credibility). Instead, I'm suggesting that one of the greatest strategies for leadership is allowing people to fail without interjecting. As a leader, never make the mistake of robbing people of the blessing of learning from their mistakes. If you don't allow them to make mistakes, they'll never have those learning moments.

Consider the greatest lessons you ever learned. Did they come in victory or defeat? If you're anything like me, the pain of defeat was a greater teacher than the pride of victory.

I didn't start to get into shape until my children asked me to jump on the trampoline with them and I couldn't. I didn't hire a coach in my financial planning practice until I was so broke and desperate that it was my last resort before quitting. I didn't learn to be a better husband and father until my wife and I went through a separation.

Look, I didn't enjoy any of that at the time, but I wouldn't be who I am today without those incredible learning moments. I'm often asked, "Ryan, if you could do something over again in your life, what would it be?" I understand the spirit of the question, but the reality is that I wouldn't do anything over again. I've been in some extremely uncomfortable situations and circumstances. I wish it didn't have to be that way, but it does. So get used to it . . . for yourself and for others.

Besides, I don't believe for a second that those who constantly attempt to save others from their mistakes are only after those people's best interests. No, I think more often than not, they're after their own self-preservation. It stings to watch someone else suffer, but suffering is a great teacher.

Have you ever watched a speech so painful that you personally felt embarrassed? Or a stand-up comedy routine that was so bad you laughed out loud to break the tension? Those are self-defense techniques. You feel awkward, so you do something to feel less awkward.

Ask yourself, "Am I trying to serve others when I rescue them, or am I trying to serve myself?"

Leadership is painful. You're going to have to bite your tongue and watch people suffer. That's why leadership requires strength. It's not for the faint of heart.

There is one powerful strategy I've learned for allowing other people to fail: ask questions.

I run a Facebook group of roughly seventy-eight thousand people. I'm amazed how often someone will ask for some guidance or direction and be met with hundreds of comments about what to do. That's not the surprising part. What's surprising is how few commenters are willing to ask any sort of probing or follow-up questions.

How is it possible for so many men to know exactly what advice to give regarding a very specific scenario they only learned about from a few short sentences on Facebook? Spoiler alert: it isn't.

Look, if you truly want to serve others and lead, stop telling them what to do. Stop rescuing them. Stop solving their problems and find a way to help them solve their own. Any advice you give another person will always be seen through a lens of separation. They won't fully buy into what you're suggesting. But if you learn to guide people through their own problems and so they can formulate their own answers, they will buy in completely. And you will capture the influence you desire.

WRAP UP

I understand the desire to be a hero to others. I really do. It's hard to watch people struggle when you feel like you have the answer to what ails them. The truth is that although you *might* actually have the solution, men need to resist the urge to save others (again, unless there is imminent danger involved).

At the end of the day, you can't spend your precious time, energy, and resources saving people who aren't willing to participate in the rescue—your attempts will be futile.

When you do attempt to rescue others, not only is there an unnecessary risk to yourself and those you could be leading and serving, but there is an unnecessary risk to those you're trying to save.

Consider the stories we've all heard of some well-intentioned person who attempts to rescue an injured animal. The reality is that many of the animals rescued never return to the wild. They are crippled and incapable of surviving on their own. For the rest of their lives, they are dependent on others to take care of them.

Several years ago, I visited a local zoo. As my family and I walked around, we anxiously came to the lion's cage. We looked around for a minute as we tried to find the magnificent king of the jungle. After a bit of searching, one of my children excitedly exclaimed, "There he is!" I peeked in the back corner of the cage and saw the most pathetic feline I had ever seen. He was casually resting on his man-made perch with a sadness in his eyes that, in the darkest moments of my life, I had become all too familiar with. This would-be king was physically weak, malnourished, and quite a sorry sight to behold.

I couldn't help but think that he had completely resigned any hope of becoming the beast he was meant to be. Maybe he was just tired.

Regardless, when I look into the eyes of so many men and women I deal with on a daily basis, I see the same thing. They're lost, afraid, and broken. While I think any man who has the desire to serve others might feel a level of sympathy when confronted with one of those individuals, we must resist the urge to save them else they too become like the neutered lion I encountered in the zoo that day.

Your job as a man isn't to save others. Your job is to lead them. Where women are generally more equipped to comfort, empathize, and nurture those who are feeling down, men are generally more equipped to inspire, ignite the fire, and challenge others to rise up.

Besides, who are you to rob another of the lessons that come only from experiences we'd all naturally like to avoid? Are you arrogant enough to believe that *you* know what is best for another? Are you so selfish that you would strip from them an opportunity to learn, grow, and develop in failure?

Where heroes rescue those who are incapable of saving themselves, masculine leadership empowers others to develop the frameworks, mindset, and skills to do things on their own.

RULES FOR NOT ACTING LIKE A SUPERHERO

1. **Be Willing to Get Dirty.** Don't be a White Knight, and don't let the desire for accolades and notoriety dictate your decisions and actions. Be willing to get your hands dirty if it means serving other people even—*especially*—when no one is looking. You're going to get banged up as you do. You're not immune to the danger of leadership. Be sure you're doing it for the right reasons.

2. **Be a Lighthouse, Not a Tugboat.** You are meant to shine. You cannot serve people effectively if you're struggling to move, pull, push, tug, and manipulate others to where you *think* they should go. You are a grown man. Most of the people you deal with (barring your children) are grown adults. Let them make their own decisions. Stand and shine as an example of how to be, and do not leave your post.

3. **Let Others Fail.** Failure is a great teacher. Do not rob others of the blessings of failure. Yes, it sucks to see someone you care about flail around as they struggle with their challenges. But challenges make people strong. Be a lighthouse and show them the way. Do not pull them to safety (unless there is imminent danger). The best way to lead in these moments is to help people find their own solutions, not to solve everything for them.

CHAPTER SIX

LEAD BEFORE THE TITLE

No man will make a great leader who wants to do it all
himself or get all the credit for doing it.

—*Andrew Carnegie*

Many men tend to wait for permission to assume the role of leader. I'm not sure if that's biologically hardwired into us or if society has largely conditioned us to do so.

Consider that from the time we're little boys, we're constantly reminded to sit down, shut up, color within the lines, and be "good little boys." If you couple that with the growing sentiment in society that men are nothing more than sperm donors and that women are as capable as men of filling traditional male roles, it's easy to see why so many men are lost when it comes to leadership.

On one hand, men feel called to lead (and are biologically constructed to do so), but on the other, they are concerned (due to their social conditioning) that they may be mocked, ridiculed, and chastised for daring to step into what calls to them so deeply.

What's ironic is that so many feel this way. They're waiting for someone to step up. They're waiting for the right moment. They're waiting for permission.

Why? If all the men are sitting around waiting, is it not safe to assume that the man who finally decides to assert himself in the presence of passive men is the one who becomes the leader among them?

"Oh, but Ryan, what makes that man any more qualified to lead others?" the timid will gripe. The answer is that he had the balls to do it. If you felt you were qualified to lead others, why did you sit around so long, waiting for someone else to do it?

For this reason, I often ignore criticism from the cheap seats. You'd be amazed how often someone who is doing less than I am has the audacity to scold me regarding the way I grow my business, lead my family, and attempt to add value to the world.

I don't fault a man for acknowledging what he sees wrong, but if he really had anything worth sharing with me, he'd be standing alongside me in the arena doing the work. But so many men aren't. And because they're not willing to, they've forfeited their right, in my eyes, to armchair quarterback what another man is doing to assert himself.

I know you'd like the corner office overlooking the city with a fancy scripted title on your front door and a plaque on your desk with the phrase, "Name, CEO of XYZ Company." I always have, too. It isn't wrong to have that desire. It is wrong, however, to believe that someone is magically going to bestow it upon you because you hope they will. Hope, as we all know, is not an effective strategy.

The propensity to lead comes well before the title. The title comes only after you've proven yourself worthy of it.

So, if you truly want something, go get it. No excuses. No lies. No passivity. Prove you deserve it. Interestingly enough, when you do, the title takes a back seat to the true influence, authority, and credibility you have with others.

FILL THE VOIDS

I used to get so upset by the ineptness of others. I would often complain (mostly internally) about what I thought they should be doing and how horrible they were at performing their duties. It's extremely frustrating to watch someone in a position of authority perform so poorly, especially when their performance deeply impacts your life.

I'm often confronted by men who struggle with the same problem I used to have. "Ryan, I have a horrible boss or team leader. How do I deal with him?" Deal with him? You can *influence* him, but you certainly cannot *change* a person who is possibly set in his ways. But why would you want to anyway? Instead, when dealing with a difficult boss, look for the gaps they leave (and they do leave plenty).

I know, because I used to be one of those bosses. I would browbeat employees into compliance. I often neglected to care for them as people and the personal issues they were dealing with because I was so fixated on my objective that I could not see anything else. I railroaded anyone who got in my way, and I left a lot of collateral damage in my wake. As a result, my employees did not want to work for me. Sure, they wanted a paycheck, but that became the extent of our relationship: a paycheck—nothing less, nothing more.

It wasn't until I made one of my employees cry that I finally realized the error of my ways. This young woman (we'll call her Judy) was typically an incredibly driven and focused employee, excited about the job. I became frustrated with her work one day—it wasn't like her to leave messes everywhere, neglect the customers who came into the store, and slack off on her duties and responsibilities. I chastised her, only to be met with her tears before she ran into the back room, unable to deal with my inappropriate (and ineffective) approach to her performance.

More frustrated than before, I watched as another employee, moved to comfort and console an obviously very distraught young woman, followed Judy into the back room. I later found out that Judy was dealing with the death of a very close family member. Looking back, I wish I had displayed a bit more kindness and sympathy for her and the situation she was facing.

Regardless, I was impressed with the other employee's ability to diffuse the tension in that moment and do what needed to be done. Leadership. I didn't ask him to do that. I didn't assign him the task of getting Judy back on track. There were no prompts and no instructions given. What he recognized was that in the absence of proper leadership, there was an opportunity to serve. In hindsight, it isn't any surprise to me that this man gradually elevated his position of authority and the influence he had with others. Eventually, he ended up managing his own store.

In his book *Beyond Order: 12 More Rules for Life*, Jordan Peterson offers Rule 4: "Notice that opportunity lurks where responsibility has been abdicated."

The answer to the question, "How do I deal with a bad boss/team leader?" is simple: you look for opportunities. They're there, hiding in the voids others leave behind. Sometimes difficult to recognize, but they exist all the same. You'll see them if you look. If, however, you wait for others to fill the voids, you'll either be left waiting or resigned to watching others do what you should have done all along.

The great news is that you need no authority or influence over others to do so. Both will be established as you look for the opportunity to assume responsibility where little or none already exists. *That* is leading before the title.

LEADERSHIP IS RISKY

I'm fairly certain the reason most men don't lead isn't because they don't see the opportunities to do so, but because they're afraid to. Few are willing to admit that, however, because men "aren't supposed to be scared." But if you aren't willing to admit you're afraid, how in the world do you expect to confront and defeat what stands in your way to effective leadership?

Only when a man is courageous enough to acknowledge that he is afraid does he have the potential to arm himself with the mindset and skill sets to deal with the fear. Courage isn't the absence of fear, but the ability to drive on in the face of it. It's okay to acknowledge your fear—you probably should.

Think about why the feeling of fear even exists. It's there to serve you, right? A healthy dose of fear keeps you and others out of compromising situations. The problem is that the brain has a difficult time differentiating between the fear that keeps you alive and the fear that keeps you from growing past your comfort zone.

If you find yourself in a dangerous place, your fear kicks in and alerts you that maybe you ought to get yourself out of that environment. If, on the other hand, you're feeling afraid because you have to give a speech to a group of investors in your company, it will likely drive you to be more prepared to land that presentation. Both types of fear drive you to action. One drives you to flee; one drives you to fight.

Fear alone isn't enough. You must interpret the fear you're feeling. Is it keeping you safe or keeping you complacent? If safety is an issue, caution is warranted. But moving forward in the face of complacency is always encouraged. Leadership is risky, which is why so few are willing to assume the role and the responsibility that comes with it. But with enough knowledge and insight, any man can assert himself as the leader he wishes to be.

Here are the most common pitfalls to avoid on your path to leadership—actions that ultimately undermine influence, authority, and credibility, rather than bolster it:

- Offering unsolicited feedback
- Undermining the boss
- Putting your own interests first
- Falsely claiming credibility

Offering unsolicited feedback

Has there ever been a time in the history of mankind when someone has actually appreciated unsolicited feedback? I know it's challenging for us, as men, to resist recommending solutions to problems when they're so glaringly obvious.

Whether your wife is trying to tell you about how bad her day was, a teammate is venting at work, or a boss is upset about a problem with the organization, I urge you to resist rushing in to offer a solution. There are several reasons for this.

1. The other party may not actually be interested in solutions. They may simply be looking to blow off steam. If you bombard them with potential options, it's only going to elevate their stress, not alleviate it.

2. You may not know the entire picture. You're catching a glimpse of the challenge someone else is dealing with. Don't rush into a trap you know nothing about.

3. It's not your place. Frankly, no one asked you, and it doesn't really matter why. You may not have earned enough influence, authority, and credibility with others to offer feedback to a situation you know very little about. Don't undermine yourself with a superhero complex.

Undermining the boss

Please don't misinterpret my recommendation to "lead before the title" to mean "undermine your boss." It's easy to do, especially considering that your boss might be a bumbling buffoon incapable of leading others effectively. If you have one of these bosses, I suggest you allow them to dig their own grave (trust me, he or she will with time). There isn't a thing you need to do to expedite the process.

Inevitably, when I'm chastising one of my children, my oldest seems to be under the impression that I need his help or that he's their father. Frequently, I have to remind him, "Don't get yourself in the middle of other people's problems. Stay clear and away from danger unless absolutely necessary."

Ultimately, your job is to edify and support your boss, leader, team manager, owner, coach, etc. I know how challenging that can be, but this is *the* best course of action. Make your boss look good. Give him credit where appropriate. And help him or her achieve his goals. A truly incompetent boss won't last, and a lackluster boss might just rise to the challenge.

Putting your own interests first

Forgetting that you're here to serve others is the quickest way to undermine what you're working so tirelessly to develop. It may seem like you'll need to place your own needs above others' in order to lead effectively. While it's true that you do need to take care yourself, never make the mistake of thinking that your subordinates exist to serve you. They don't. You exist to serve them—that is, if you want to be an effective leader.

Instead, look for opportunities to create win-win scenarios—situations in which your values, needs, and desires align with your team's, rather than work against them.

Many people exist in a world of false dichotomies. They falsely assume that for one situation to exist (you getting ahead), it *has* to come at the expense of others (their falling behind). This isn't true. As the great Zig Ziglar once said, "You can have everything in life you want, if you will just help other people get what they want."

This isn't the exception; it's the rule. The more you help others get what they're after . . .

- Your wife, to feel honored and cherished for who she is
- Your children, the love and attention of their father
- Your employees, meaningful and well-paying work
- Your neighbors, a safe, enjoyable community to live in
- Your coworkers, job satisfaction and growth opportunities

. . . the more you're going to uncover and unlock exactly what it is you're after.

Falsely claiming credit

Resist the urge to be a blowhard. I'm reminded of President Trump as I write this section. Regardless of how you feel about him, it was apparent that both during and after his presidency, legacy and social media outlets painted him as the villain. Often, Trump would suggest that since the media wasn't willing to promote him in a positive light to even the slightest degree, he felt *he* had to do all the promotion.

While he had varying degrees of success with a subsection of the population, self-promotion often falls on deaf ears and ends up calling into question the character, validity, and competency of the self-promoter.

It's easy to claim that you're God's gift. It may even work—for a while. Eventually, though, people will catch on, and they'll be turned off. Whatever influence you might have garnered will slip through your fingers.

Instead, I suggest letting your work speak for itself. Don't get me wrong, there is a time and place for self-promotion, but if you can't ever get to the point where your results are doing the speaking for you, you might want to check yourself and ask if you're really doing the work you're capable of.

Where self-promotion only goes so far, your results and the word of other influential, credible people will take it the rest of the way.

WRAP UP

Here's the truth: everyone wants to be a leader; few are willing to lead.

The title of leader seems to be what so many men are after. While the title can certainly be alluring, it only goes so far. The title will garner you compliance. True leadership, however, will garner you commitment.

Most people complain about the lack of leadership in modern society. We blame our bosses, community leaders, and politicians for what ails us. We often cry that others aren't solving our problems, and pontificate about how, if given the chance, we could do a better job. Well, prove it! There has never been a better time to step up and prove that you can do a better job.

That's the bright side of the current lack of leadership. Where all the average man sees is a void, the man who truly has the ability to influence others sees a way to fill it. We, as men, have a tremendous opportunity to fill those voids and serve those who would love nothing more than to be led righteously to a place they could not have imagined going on their own.

Instead of measuring your level of leadership by the sophistication of your title, measure it by the human capital you have with others. That's what really matters.

Imagine walking into your local bank and approaching the closest teller. When you get there, you ask, "How much money can I pull out of my bank account?" The teller responds, "Let's take a look." She then pulls up your bank account to check the balance. If you have $50,000 in your bank account, you can pull out no more than $50,000. Period.

Human capital works very much the same way. You cannot pull out of others what you have not put in. Regardless of whether you possess the title, unless you're willing to invest in others, they will never be fully vested in you.

But here's the good news: You don't need the title. You don't need permission. You don't need the okay from a boss to lead others.

You need only an opportunity and the testicular fortitude to capitalize on it. I say "testicular fortitude" because there is risk involved. There always is anytime a man chooses to exert himself. Others are going to try to tear you down. Some people will see you as a threat. Hell, you'll even sabotage yourself from time to time because you let your own selfish desires get in the way of serving others.

But remember, in the absence of vision, inspiration, communication, and direction lies opportunity—and frankly, the moral obligation to do something about it.

RULES FOR LEADING BEFORE THE TITLE

1. **Fill the Voids Others Leave.** Instead of complaining about the ineptness of others, be grateful for it. Look for opportunities where others have shirked it. There are plenty of them available if you *stop and look*. Don't ever fall prey to the "it's not my responsibility" mentality.

Instead, look for meaningful work to become your responsibility. This is what all great leaders do.

2. **Embrace the Risks of Leadership and Hedge against Them.** Don't be afraid. Or more accurately, don't let your fear of leadership keep you from leading. We're all afraid. If you can learn to appreciate that most people are looking for others to lead them, you can develop immense influence and authority with them—and reap the rewards that come with those things. That said, don't be stupid. Embrace the risks involved, but be intelligent about the way you deal with them. You don't need to become a martyr to be a leader.

3. **Focus on Human Capital, Not a Title.** It's tempting to chase the title. We're often led to believe it's the title that defines us. A title might buy you some temporary authority, but it will not create lasting influence and credibility. Focus on serving others. Build your network. Help others solve their own problems. Make the connections people need. Make yourself indispensable. When you do, the title won't matter—you'll know it and so will everyone else.

CHAPTER SEVEN

RENDER YOURSELF OBSOLETE

A leader is best when people barely know he exists . . .
when his work is done, his aim fulfilled, they will say:
"We did it ourselves."

—Lao Tzu

'm often asked by first-time fathers for "the best piece of fatherhood advice." Sure, I could give the standard answers:

- Love your children unconditionally
- Don't neglect your wife
- Teach your kids X,Y, and Z
- Help out around the house while your wife recovers
- Try to get some sleep
- Etc., etc., etc.

None of those answers are necessarily wrong, but there is only one answer that lies at the foundation of what it means to be an effective father (and a leader in general). My response to these men is always, "Never forget, it's now your job to put yourself out of work."

That's the uncomfortable truth about leadership so many men are unwilling to acknowledge—that it isn't about leading perpetually. In fact, if your people (family, friends, colleagues, coworkers, etc.) cannot function without you there, you are the antithesis of a leader, not the embodiment of it.

It's painful, however, to know that you should be actively working to put yourself out of a job. Last year, I took my oldest boys to a high school basketball game. I was flattered that they still wanted to spend time with me and jumped at the opportunity to take them.

We got to the game, grabbed some snacks at the concession stand, and made our way to our seats. Within five minutes of sitting down, and after wolfing down their pretzels and hotdogs, my sons anxiously asked if they could go find their buddies. "Sure," I responded. I spent the next couple of hours alone at the half-court line, watching the game by myself. This was the first time they didn't want to sit with their dad.

Periodically, I'd scan the gym to find the boys. I typically found them on the upper level, running around with their friends, working feverishly to catch the attention of the young ladies who were working feverishly to catch the attention of the young men.

As I sat there, a little saddened that my sons had outgrown sitting in the stands with me, I remembered that this process was good and right and true. It's natural for them to seek, find, and work toward their independence. Although it stings to know that I am not needed as much as I once was, I do take pride in knowing they are comfortable and resilient enough to leave the safe nest my wife and I provide.

The alternative is to raise dependent children who are incapable of making decisions on their own or providing for themselves as they become adults. Unfortunately, it is not uncommon in culture today to find young men and ladies who are so immature—mentally, physically, and emotionally—that they cannot fathom leading their own lives.

What we see in the workforce often mirrors what we see on the home front. I have talked with thousands of business owners over the past ten years who are finding it increasingly difficult to find employees worth their weight. It's become like pulling teeth to find assertive, self-driven workers willing and able to do their jobs, take initiative, and lead themselves, let alone a task they are assigned at work.

Unfortunately, we've done this to ourselves. We have become so self-absorbed, and life has become so convenient, that we have failed to do what is necessary to teach others how to lead themselves.

DO WHAT IS PRUDENT, NOT WHAT IS COMFORTABLE

My friend, Pete Roberts, founder and CEO of the mixed martial-arts products company Origin USA, once explained a very interesting concept to me regarding the more than two hundred people he employs. He said, "Ryan, when it comes to people in the workforce, you have squatters, renters, and owners."

He then went on to explain that squatters work to get the most while giving the least in return. They'll hang around only as long as they're getting more than what they're giving. They're a strain on the system and must be identified and removed from the team.

Renters are different. Renters are good workers. They will show up on time, do the work you ask of them, do it well, and punch out right as their shift ends. When they're done with work, they're done. They don't take it home with them. They don't put in extra hours and don't look for ways to expand the business or their own capabilities. They're reliable but don't typically go above and beyond.

Owners are the best type of worker. They are fully vested in the job and the mission of the work. They constantly look for ways to improve themselves and the efficacy of the processes, systems, tools, and resources inside the organization. These types of employees are an investment and, even if they leave the organization at some point, what they contribute to it far outweighs the resources that went into training and compensating them.

Pete considers it his job to build owners, not renters and certainly not squatters, for his team.

But there is a challenge when it comes to owners. Owners take time, attention, and financial capital to build. Building owners isn't easy, and it doesn't happen overnight.

In a fast-paced, competitive environment with so much on the line, it's tempting to invest the bare minimum and put people to work *right now*. While we can all see the appeal of doing that in the short term, it certainly doesn't play out well in the long term. But the long term is where it pays to be prudent.

So, if we can acknowledge that the benefits of building owners outweigh the challenges, why don't we put more effort into it? One primary reason: we are afraid of confrontation.

Consider how many discussions, course corrections, and hours of training are required to shift someone from a squatter or renter mentality to an owner mentality. It's painstaking, frustrating work, and it's often met with resistance from the other party.

There are very few people who like to be pushed out of their comfort zones, but that's exactly what is required for effective leadership.

You have to be willing to make yourself and others uncomfortable.

To go back to parenting, imagine what it would be like if you handed everything to your children on a silver platter. We all know of entitled, spoiled, sniveling brats, but we don't think our children would ever be like that. Yet, if we don't offer them the resistance required to become self-sustaining, independent adults, that's exactly how things will play out.

You know what you want from your children, players, coworkers, and employees. You know what it will take to get them there. Are you willing to do what is necessary to make it so?

If you're not, you're not a leader. You may be sitting in a leadership position, but you're not leading correctly or effectively.

It can be painful to offer constructive criticism to your employees during their annual reviews. It hurts to have to correct your children or watch them suffer as they live with the consequences of their choices. It's hard to watch others clumsily stumble through a task, assignment, or project, knowing that you could easily relieve them of their discomfort if you did it yourself.

In the moment, they may appreciate you for taking over the task. But because they never learned the lessons they needed to, they'll struggle harder down the road. And then, they'll harbor resentment and animosity toward you for robbing them of prudent leadership when they needed it most.

Although tough love might be painful, those under your leadership will grow to respect the man who honors them, helps them see what could possibly be, and sets them on the path to realize their full potential. And *you* can take pride in being an effective leader.

TRUST OTHERS, TRUST YOURSELF

Building owners requires humility because you're going to have to let go of all the things you took pride in doing yourself. And I know how hard it can be to let go of your "baby" (literally and figuratively).

I started the *Order of Man* podcast in 2015 with nothing more than an eighty-dollar microphone, the four-year-old computer I was already using, and a desk from the 1960s in the spare bedroom of our house. It took me eight months of work to earn our first dime and years to reach our first million podcast listeners. I kicked and clawed and scrapped every step of the way to make what many thought was wasted effort worth something meaningful to millions of men.

I remember when I realized I was in over my head with *Order of Man* and that, in order to grow to the level I desired, I was going to need some additional help.

Our exclusive brotherhood, the Iron Council (see appendix), had just reached eighty-three members, and as I thought about how I could serve the men who had invested their hard-earned money with us, I couldn't help but acknowledge that we had lost some of the intimacy of our brotherhood. Hell, there were members invested in me whose names I didn't even know.

It was hard to conclude that maybe it was time to enlist some help. But I decided that, in order to maintain the personalized attention, I would ask ten men inside the Council to become Battle Team Leaders. This meant they would be running their own teams of five to ten men, and I would be giving them authority to act on my and the Council's behalf.

That was a hard day. But it was also a cathartic day for me. I realized that even though I had subscribed to the mantra, "If you want it done right, you have to do it yourself," for most of my life, it just wasn't true. There were incredibly talented, gifted individuals willing and eager to step up to the challenge of leadership.

The only thing that kept them from doing so was an egocentric leader (myself) bottlenecking the entire process and the results that would come with it. Since then, the Iron Council has grown to over thirteen hundred members representing every continent on this planet. We now have more than seventy teams, each with its own Battle Team Leader leading twelve to fifteen men.

What would the Iron Council look like now if I had continued to stand in the way? I can't imagine it would be the powerhouse that it is. As incredible as it is now, that didn't come from me standing at the helm, dictating, directing, and micromanaging every minute detail of our day-to-day operations. No, it came from me getting out of the way and learning how to empower others on their own journey to masculine leadership.

Gentlemen, at some point in your life (if you have any hope of growth beyond what you're currently experiencing), you're going to have to face the reality that you might be your own greatest hindrance. You're also going to have to accept that there are people out there who are better at certain things than you are. In other words, you're going to have to trust.

Think about it for a minute. You trust yourself enough to know that, faced with a challenging situation, you can rise above it. Can you not see that others are capable of doing the same? Of course they are. And, if you want to build influence with others, trust is the bedrock for it.

You're going to have to develop the faith that others can learn. They can adapt. They can evolve. Same as you.

LEADERS BUILD LEADERS, NOT FOLLOWERS

Social media has ruined us in a lot of ways. For everything I love about it (and there is a lot I love about it), the medium has some very real flaws and presents very real challenges. For one, tracking your follower count can consume you. It's plastered everywhere. The insights typically offered in business accounts emphasize that the rate of growth in your accounts is the single most important metric. While growth in your online presence certainly represents some level of interest in the information you're putting out into the world, it does very little to distinguish whether a man is leading in any sort of effective way.

Some of the largest accounts on social media have feeds filled with nothing more than ridiculous, crude memes designed more to entertain than to educate and empower (which are better metrics of illustrating leadership than how many people happen to be following you).

Many people are consumed with surface-level metrics outside of social media as well. They prioritize things that have very little to do with leading with influence, authority, and credibility. What kind of car do you drive? What neighborhood do you live in? How big is your house? What kind of clothes do you wear?

While these metrics may offer clues into how you are showing up as a leader, they don't even scratch the surface regarding your ability to lead others effectively.

Both the digital and the tangible world are more concerned with your followers than they are with how many leaders you've created. And your ability to develop leaders is a vastly better indication of what type of leader you are than how many people (many of whom can be bought both digitally and tangibly) "follow" you.

I've often heard notable online personas brag about how many followers—or even worse, "fans"—they have. Leaders don't want fans. Leaders work to empower people.

In all fairness, if you consider it your job to entertain the masses (which does have some value), I guess follower/fan count would be the metric to track.

But that isn't what *you're* after. Leadership has never been about entertaining the masses. Sure, your delivery and your ability to captivate others is important, but entertainment is a means, not the end.

The mob is easy to entertain, especially in this age. I can easily lie, cheat, and steal my way to notoriety. The same cannot be said about garnering influence, credibility, and authority with others. Those *must* be earned.

If you're going to focus on a metric, I would suggest that the better, more accurate representation of your ability to lead is how many leaders you've groomed and empowered.

I learned this very early in my retail career. My first job in retail was at a Journeys shoe store. Over several years, I worked my way from part-time employee to store manager. As I did, I began to get the attention of other stores in the mall that I worked in (this is the way of the "mall rat"—to bounce around from store to store in search of better pay and/or opportunity). One store with an eye on me was Buckle.

I had applied there when I was just a sales associate with Journeys but was denied a job. Now, the store manager for Buckle was actively recruiting me.

Long story short, the store manager of Buckle made me an offer I could not refuse: entry into their managerial training program. I accepted and started my training.

My time at Journeys was very cutthroat. I felt that as a leader, I needed to outproduce everyone (which I consistently did). I would often schedule myself for the busiest times and outwork everyone on the sales floor to consistently produce the highest sales numbers.

But when I moved to Buckle, something was very different. My store manager, whom I deeply respected, began to show me a better, more effective way of leading. I really enjoyed sales (I still do). The process of starting with someone who doesn't know a thing about you and getting them to trust you enough to buy something has always been fascinating to me.

My store manager at Buckle, however, taught me that the measure of your leadership is not how much you can personally sell, but how much you can empower other people to sell and how much your store produces in general.

But there was another metric she took pride in. She was exceptionally good at developing leaders, getting them promoted, and moving them to different stores.

I started at Buckle in St. George, Utah. Not long after that, I moved to Orem, Utah, to help open a new store in University Place (previously University Mall), and not long after that, I moved with my new bride to Rancho Cucamonga, California, to open my *own* store in the newly constructed Victoria Gardens Mall.

Looking back, the people I hold in the highest regard are the ones who did everything they could—not to beat me, but to empower me on my own path of growth and progress.

Leadership is selfless, not selfish. When you learn to empower others, your needs will be served—not because you're consumed with what you'll get, but because you're focused on what you can give.

And, giving will *always* garner more influence, authority, and credibility with others than taking. If you want to be a leader, keep better track of the leaders you've influenced, not the followers you've created.

WRAP UP

Leaders don't trip over themselves. Leaders don't get in the way and, consequently, trip others up. Leaders coach, mentor, and nurture. But above all, leaders inspire others to lead.

I understand how difficult that can be. The most challenging aspect is illustrated in the mindset we often hear in the corporate environment: "I'm just training my competition."

It might be true that if you focus more on developing leaders than followers, your people will, at some point, set out on their own and no longer need you.

Frankly, it's bittersweet to see my children or members of the Iron Council (or anyone I wish to serve, for that matter) strike out on their own and seemingly forget about what I did for them on their path to independence. But it's important that we acknowledge that leaders don't lead for the accolades or recognition. If we did, follower counts would exclusively be what would matter. No, leaders lead because it's the right thing to do. Any leader worth his weight derives his value not on dependence on him, but on the ability of others to lead in his absence.

I vividly remember the first time I asked one of our Battle Team Leaders on the Iron Council to host one of our Friday calls (something I had previously reserved only for myself). As hesitant as I was to relinquish the control of my responsibility, I later learned that not only did the man who hosted the call do a tremendous job, but there were hundreds of men who gained incredible insight in a way I never could have delivered myself. At first, I was upset. But the moment I stopped and considered that the man I asked to lead the call was someone I personally acknowledged, trained, and promoted was the moment I found a new sense of pride in building leaders, not followers.

Besides, the drive to push or keep others down and prop ourselves up is derived from a sense of fear. And fear (or any emotion, for that matter) is not something men base their decisions on. (Emotion is *a* consideration; not the only consideration.)

If you're afraid that someone might replace you or that your children might forget you, you're operating from a place of scarcity, and you will never realize your full potential as a husband, father, business owner, and/or community leader. In fact, if this describes you, not only are you not a leader, but you are an anti-leader, more concerned with limiting people's potential than revealing and realizing it.

RULES FOR RENDERING YOURSELF OBSOLETE

1. **Make Decisions Based on What Is Right, Not What Is Comfortable.** Comfort is enticing. But making decisions based on what is most

comfortable is what everyone does. You don't want to be like most people. You want to lead. Making the difficult choices few are willing to make will set you apart from everyone else. It's going to sting at first, but like anything in life, choosing the harder path now will make things easier down the road. Choosing the easy path now will make everything else harder than it needs to be later on.

2. Trust That Others Can Perform . . . If You Empower Them. It's hard to let go of the things you care so much about. But your unwillingness to enlist the help of others is arrogant and limits your growth. You have the ability to become a powerful force multiplier if you learn to enlist the help of others. Drop the ego. Drop the pride. Recruit, train, and inspire a team of powerhouses, and you'll not only foster a deep sense of trust and credibility with others, but you'll outperform all the men out there who think they have to do it alone.

3. Build Leaders, Not Followers. Jocko Willink introduced millions of people to the concept of decentralized command. So many would-be leaders believe it's their job to do everything. It isn't. I don't respect a leader who feels like he has to do it all. All he becomes is a bottleneck on the path toward victory. I do, however, respect a leader who has the capacity to build and develop other leaders and remove himself from the equation. If your people need you around to function, you're a manager, not a leader. If you equip and empower them to lead in their own lives (both personally and professionally), you're on the path to masculine leadership. Don't be threatened by your people's success. If you are, you're more of a threat than they are.

PART III

HARNESS MASCULINITY FOR PRODUCTIVE OUTCOMES

Being a male is a matter of birth. Being a man is a matter of choice.

—Edwin Louis Cole

Masculinity is amoral. It's neither good nor bad, productive nor destructive. It simply is. I know plenty of people would argue otherwise. On one side of the spectrum, you have those who would tell you that masculinity is inherently good. It's not. It has the power to be good, but it is not inherently good. (Manliness, yes. Masculinity, no.) On the other hand, you have those who would argue that masculinity is inherently bad. It's not. It has the power to be bad, but it is not inherently bad.

This is why I don't subscribe to the term "toxic masculinity." Masculinity, by definition, is not toxic. Masculinity is defined as qualities or attributes regarded as characteristics of men—nothing more, nothing less. There is no judgment in that definition. It is pretty straightforward. And who gets to decide "attributes regarded as characteristics of men"? Biology and culture. That's it. "See!" some of my critics will shout. "Masculinity is a social construct!" No, that's not what I'm saying at all. Masculinity, as I mentioned in previous chapters, is a biological construct, and, collectively/societally, we've decided to support the biological construct of not only masculinity, but femininity as well.

So, let's address this concept of toxic masculinity before we go any further, since it seems to be such a polarizing subject and I'd like to set the record straight once and for all.

I understand what some people are trying to say when they use the term. You might understand my previous statement to mean that if masculinity is amoral, it has the potential to become toxic. While I agree that men can and have throughout history used masculinity to harm others, it is not inherently or exclusively in men's nature to do so. Both women and men have the propensity for injustice toward others (although often exercised differently. Interestingly, though, you never hear about "toxic femininity.").

Regardless, a man can use his propensity for violence to do grave injustices to other individuals as easily as another man can use his propensity for violence to protect his property and his loved ones.

But there are plenty of individuals who would use the term "toxic" to describe all masculinity. The American Psychological Association

(APA) has stated in *CE Corner* (a collection of continuing education articles offered by the APA's Office of CE in Psychology) that "the main thrust of the subsequent research is that traditional masculinity—marked by stoicism, competitiveness, dominance, and aggression—is, on the whole, harmful."[1]

The APA, by its own admission, is responsible for, among other things, "elevating the public's understanding of, regard for, and use of psychology, preparing the discipline and profession of psychology for the future, and strengthening the APA's standings as the authoritative voice for psychology." In other words, the APA is responsible for the way millions of psychologists view, clinically diagnose, and treat boys and men.

That's a pretty strong entity suggesting that masculinity is inherently toxic.

So I reject the term. I don't qualify masculinity with terms like "toxic," "dangerous," or "destructive." Conversely, I don't qualify masculinity with positive terms like "healthy," "productive," or "honorable." Masculinity just is.

And since that's the case, it's not our masculinity that defines us as men, but, rather, how we use it—what I refer to as "manliness." So why didn't I call this book *The Manliness Manifesto*? I didn't call it that because I actually wanted to address the way that we, as men, can harness the power of masculinity for productive outcomes for ourselves and those we care about.

There is no escaping our masculinity. And contrary to popular belief, it isn't something we should be consumed with escaping, anyway. It's our ability to be masculine that has quite literally created more freedom, independence, and sovereignty than any other factor in the history of mankind.

As fire can destroy, it also can cleanse and clear the way for new things to grow.

In my first book, *Sovereignty: The Battle for the Hearts and Minds of Men*, I dedicated an entire section of the book (Part III) to a "Code of Conduct" men can utilize to gain absolute control over their hearts and minds. In that section, I laid out thirteen virtues every man can utilize to recapture his sovereignty:

- Self-reliance
- Intentionality
- Discernment
- Wisdom
- Ownership
- Strength
- Humility
- Integrity
- Conviction
- Self-awareness
- Discipline
- Mastery
- Courage

While I don't discount any of the virtues I covered in that book, we need to dig a bit deeper into who we are as men. The thirteen virtues I listed and discussed in my previous book serve their purpose. But let's be honest, you can find a thousand books on why discipline (or any of the thirteen virtues I listed) is crucial to your self-development journey.

In this book, however, I decided that I wanted to dive deep into who we are as men and what makes us men in the first place. While it would have been easier for me to write a book about discipline, ownership, humility, and/or integrity, it's long overdue that we discuss what really sets us apart as men and some of the virtues many are unwilling to touch. We'll start with what the APA deems "harmful."

- Stoicism
- Competitiveness
- Dominance
- Aggression

To round things out, we'll cover four other virtues men major in that, if used correctly, have the ability to garner the influence, authority, and credibility of others but also help men develop a deep sense of purpose, meaning, and fulfillment in their lives.

- Vigilance
- Violence
- Honesty
- Self-Respect

Manliness and the deep sense of fulfillment you wish to have in your life aren't found in running away from who you are as a man, like so many people and organizations in modern culture would have you believe. They're found by fully embracing and embodying all that you have the potential to become—by harnessing your masculinity, not running away from it.

CHAPTER EIGHT

STOICISM

You have power over your mind—not outside events.
Realize this, and you will find strength.

—*Marcus Aurelius*

S toicism is as popular a subject today as it was two thousand years ago with some of the original adopters of the Stoic philosophy, notably the Roman philosophers Seneca and Epictetus and Emperor Marcus Aurelius.

While the Stoicism has served many men, it's also lulled others into believing that the best course of action for them to follow is to be emotionless in their pursuits and their desires. But to believe that Stoicism teaches men to put away, hide, and not be impacted by our emotions is a gross misunderstanding of what it actually is.

Contrary to popular belief, Stoicism is not about the suppression of emotions, but the understanding of them (among other things) to live a more meaningful, fulfilled life. Stoicism also teaches us to use logic and rationale as we navigate our lives. You might ask, "Is it possible to be both emotional and logical at the same time?" The answer is yes.

See, the problem with suppressing your emotions is that it's impossible. Not only is any attempt to do so futile, but it only leads to an increased likelihood that your suppressed emotions will, at some point, boil over, leading to an explosive and often catastrophic event with the people you care about.

Consider the last time you were angry about an event or circumstance at work. Who received the business end of that anger? Likely, your family—people who had nothing to do with causing it in the first place.

You might be tempted to believe that your emotions are a nuisance at best and destructive at worst. After all, what good is it to feel if it only leads to hardship and heartache for you and others? Well, that really isn't the point of the broad array of feelings you and I experience. Sure, your emotions may cause you to feel bad about a particular situation, but that's a feature, not a bug.

What I mean is that, if you're feeling the negative emotions of your performance, perhaps that's the best thing for you. Pain can serve you. Think about the child who is compelled to touch a red-hot stove. You warn him over and over again that it's dangerous. One day, he decides to ignore your caution and works up the courage to touch the stove. Obviously, the child burns his hand, but he never touches the hot stove again.

Men are interesting. I don't know what it is about us, but we have to experience pain for ourselves. Too often it seems like it's not enough to heed the warnings of others. We want to experience all the pain and suffering and torment ourselves. While it isn't necessary (or advisable), the sting of defeat can serve us well—if we allow it to.

Emotions are just indicators that something is working or failing miserably, although you may not immediately know what that is. Don't you want to know? Don't you want to know whether a particular action, behavior, or practice is serving or hindering you? I certainly do.

So rather than hide from the emotions as we often do, I suggest you embrace them. That's not always easy (or advisable) because we seem to believe there is a direct and inescapable correlation between our emotions and our responses to them (more on that in a second). For now, I want you to consider that your emotions don't, by default, dictate your actions. It may feel like they do, but that's only because you've been acting instinctively on your emotions for too long.

And, frankly, acting on your emotions alone is not manly. Feeling them? Yes. Experiencing them? Yes. Acting on them alone? No.

The gap between emotions and response seems to be smaller with women. I don't say that negatively at all. It has to do with their ability to feel what others are feeling. Women tend to major in empathy, sympathy, and nurturing. That requires them to place a heavier emphasis on how they and others are feeling in any given moment.

Conversely, men tend to major in the results, regardless of how others may feel about it. I'm notoriously bad at this. I tend to fixate on a target and end up leaving a wake of collateral damage in my path. When I reach my objective, I often look back only to see that I alienated and ostracized others and undermined my influence, authority, and credibility with them.

But make no mistake, I'm not asking you to act more like our fairer counterparts, where a heavier emphasis tends to be placed on how they and others feel. Quite the contrary. I'm asking you to widen the gap between what you feel and what you do. Careful, though—if you take it too far, you'll end up railroading and diminishing the value and worth of those you wish to lead.

The Austrian philosopher Viktor Frankl once said, "Between stimulus and response there is a space. In that space is our power to choose our response. In our response lies growth and our freedom." In other words, in that gap lies an opportunity to critically analyze the best path forward and the one that will produce the correct results for you and those you care for.

MIND THE GAP

Years ago, I got very upset with a situation in my life. To be honest, I can't remember what the situation was. Regardless, I remember being so infuriated about my circumstance that I clenched my fist and, without thinking, punched a hole through the drywall of our bedroom closet. (I don't believe this is uncommon for many men.)

My wife asked, "Why did you do that?"

"Because I'm pissed," I told her. I can't remember where the conversation went from there, but I have spent a lot of time thinking about that situation and others when I let my emotions get the better of me.

Was it true that I punched the wall because I was mad? Yes, I believe it was. Was punching the wall a required and inevitable outlet for my anger? No, I don't believe it was.

See, so often we'll excuse our behavior and write it off as the natural result of an emotion we may be experiencing. But that isn't true. Our emotions are separate from our responses to them. The only reason we feel like they are inextricably connected is because we've programmed our responses for so many years that we no longer have to exert any time thinking about whether or not they are appropriate.

But that's the problem, isn't it? Too often we fail to think, and in a moment of rage, we end up doing something that could hurt ourselves and hurt others, mentally, emotionally, or even physically.

Those emotional reactions don't exactly elicit the type of credibility we desire, and, if played out too frequently, greatly diminish our ability to lead others effectively.

People don't follow emotional leaders for the simple reason that they are irrational. We've all had a boss, manager, leader, etc., who we've seriously considered to be bipolar. One minute, he is happy as can be. The next, he's yelling at everyone. A leader must be even-keeled if he is to be respected. And you cannot be even-keeled if you lend too much credence to your emotions. That's not to say you can't use emotion to garner the respect of others (we'll talk about that shortly).

Let's not assume that to be a great leader, you must be emotionless. As we established in the last chapter, that isn't true at all.

It's asinine to believe that we can't use the broad array of emotions we experience in any given moment as a metric and factor for what we ought to do moving forward—it's just not the only factor. Other factors may include deadlines, client expectations, technological capabilities, financial resources and capital, overall goals and objectives, and the safety and well-being of others. The list of considerations is endless, and our emotions are only one of many variables.

So how do you know how much attention you ought to give to the emotions you may be experiencing? Simple. You evaluate. You spend time thinking about all that goes into the decisions you make. Armed with as much intel as possible, then and only then do you act.

Let's go back to the story I shared of me punching the wall in our closet. Did my reaction (punching the wall) do anything to move the needle in the right direction? Of course not. If anything, it moved the needle in the wrong direction. I scared my wife, and I did damage to my own property that required financial resources to correct.

Conversely, if I had given myself some space and margin (this is what I call "minding the gap"), I could have developed a plan and strategy for fixing whatever problem I was dealing with. Instead, I only compounded the problem by acting solely in anger.

As Victor Frankl said, "In our response lies growth and our freedom." A response is best formulated by minding the gap between what you're feeling and what you end up doing about it.

USING EMOTION TO INSPIRE OTHERS

There is an opportunity found in the power of emotion to inspire yourself and others. This is known as motivation.

Motivation seems to get a bad rap these days. "Motivation is bullshit," some will say. Or, "Discipline is greater than motivation." While I agree that discipline is a crucial factor when it comes to your own and others' performance, I'm not sure why anyone would ever overlook the power of motivation and inspiration. Yes, it's fleeting. And, yes, it tends to be an inferior source of fuel for keeping at a task or project for extended lengths of time. But why shouldn't we use all the tools at our disposal to accomplish our objectives and help others do the same?

Consider some of the most inspirational speeches you've ever heard:

- Martin Luther King Jr.'s "I Have a Dream"
- Winston Churchill's "We Shall Fight on the Beaches"
- Abraham Lincoln's Gettysburg Address
- George Washington's Farewell Address
- Theodore Roosevelt's "Man in the Arena"

All these men had the great insight and ability to utilize the power of emotion to stir people to righteous action. But make no mistake, none of them were being emotional. That's not what I'm suggesting.

Being emotional means you're using your emotions solely to dictate your actions. *Using* emotions, on the other hand, means you're being deliberate and intentional about how you harness your natural feelings to build trust, respect, and credibility with others. Correct action and the results that follow breed trust, respect, and credibility. If you're the man who drives people to productive action using all the means at your disposal, you will establish your influence and authority.

But you can undermine yourself if you rely too heavily on emotion. There are appropriate times to utilize or even display emotion, and there are times when it's inappropriate to do so. This is where the softness of modernity comes in. Many in society would tell you that it's always okay to express your emotion. That isn't true.

Too much emphasis on emotion can undermine your performance, as well as others'. When you're feeling emotional, I suggest you ask yourself whether your impulsive reaction or response is going to serve or hinder you and others.

If I find myself in the midst of a violent encounter, I will no doubt feel a level of fear. Fear is the normal response for anyone in danger. Fear, in this case, is not the problem. It's the fear, after all, that will drive you toward a response—hopefully a productive one.

Your fear may lead you to flee. It may lead you to comply. Or it may lead you to defend yourself—all of which could have a positive outcome. If, however, you allow the fear to paralyze you, you'll likely leave yourself and others vulnerable to something that has the potential to harm them.

Is it okay for a man in danger to crumple to the floor and sob uncontrollably, hoping the threat will dissipate? No. That would be an inappropriate reaction to emotion.

What, then, distinguishes being emotional from using emotion to serve a purpose?

Intentionality.

The default reaction to emotion is based on our natural desire to stay alive. It's the fight-or-flight phenomenon. And it is often inferior and unproductive relative to harnessing the effectiveness of emotion in the right situation.

So, you have a choice to make: Do you allow your emotions to control you, or do you learn to control your emotions? That is foundational to the concept of Stoicism. Your ability to distinguish between being emotional and using emotion will set you apart as someone who will help others get to a place they could not have imagined going on their own.

TRAPS AND TACTICS

Mastering our emotions can be one of the hardest things men have to do. Emotions are ingrained in us biologically, and we must learn to resist the primal urge to be led by them. The power lies not in suppressing them or attempting to remove them completely from our lives, but in understanding and harnessing them so we can produce for ourselves and others. Here are some traps to avoid and some tactics that will help you become more proficient in mastering your emotions.

Become Assertive

More often than not, men land on the extremes of the emotional scale. On one end, they bottle every emotion they experience, and on the other end, they display every emotion they experience. As with anything, the most effective path typically lies somewhere in between. If you tend to bottle up emotions, you're allowing them to fester, and they will eventually escape in unknowable and potentially unproductive ways. If you're too reckless with your emotions, they'll become the greatest determining factor in how you behave, which will undermine your credibility with others. People don't follow emotionally reactive leaders for long.

The best course of action is to allow yourself to experience your broad range of emotions without allowing them to control every bit of your reaction to the outside world.

Create More Margin

As I mentioned earlier, the gap between what you feel and what you do is *the* single greatest factor in how you will allow your emotions to serve you and those you wish to lead. The smaller the gap, the more reckless you'll likely be, as you will make decisions without giving yourself adequate time to consider whether those decisions constitute the best path forward.

If you feel yourself becoming overly emotional and reactionary, your best strategy is to remove yourself from the situation. Go for a walk. Go to the gym. Call a friend. Draw or paint. Play the guitar. Go for a drive.

Be careful, though. It may be tempting for you to disengage altogether. If you do that, you run the risk of bottling up your emotions. I'm not asking you to disengage completely. I'm asking you to withdraw temporarily so you can come back to the situation with a fresh perspective and a level head.

No one likes a leader who can't control his emotions or who runs away, like a coward, from his problems.

Be Intentional

Widening the margin "between stimulus and response" will allow for other considerations beyond what you're experiencing emotionally. Emotions are fleeting and fickle. If you're anything like me, one minute you may be down on yourself, and the next, you're on a complete emotional high.

This is why it's crucial that you learn to become more intentional not only about interpreting your emotions, but also about using them effectively. Emotions are tools. I could bang the shit out of my thumb with a hammer as easily as I could use it to strike a nail. Same tool, completely different outcomes.

As you're leading, ask yourself the following questions:

"What am I trying to accomplish?"

"What do others need from me?"

"What is the best way to give people what they need and help us all win?"

I've often found myself chastising one of my children only to realize I am undermining myself (and my child) by doing so. Yelling doesn't exactly elicit the type of buy-in you're looking for from others. When I stop and consider those moments between my children and myself, I know that what I really want is not to beat them into submission, but for them to learn the lesson they need to help them on their path. This is the power of intentionality. It's clear. It's deliberate. It's calculated. And it's effective.

Practice

As with anything, the best way to get good is to practice. But how do you practice Stoicism? First, you need to be aware that what you experience may or may not serve you, and that your natural inclination (fight or flight) in any given circumstance may lead you down a path you don't want to go.

But that doesn't mean you have to completely reject what you feel. In fact, I hope I've shown you that you *shouldn't* do that at all. Instead, I would suggest that you experience your feelings fully. That's right. Give yourself permission to feel whatever you feel in the moment completely. You don't need to act on it just because you feel it. But you'll never know how to harness your emotion if you don't allow yourself to experience it.

As you're *thinking* about what you *feel* (which leads to a healthy integration of logic and emotion), consider what lesson you need to learn. Consider *why* you're feeling the way you are. Most importantly, contemplate what you ought to do about it.

Then, and only then, should you act on it. The more you practice this framework—awareness, experience, thinking, acting—the better you'll get at harnessing your emotions for power, not destruction.

CHAPTER NINE

COMPETITIVENESS

Battle is the most magnificent competition in which a human being can indulge. It brings out all that is best; it removes all that is base. All men are afraid in battle. The coward is the one who lets his fear overcome his sense of duty. Duty is the essence of manhood.

—George S. Patton

I t's hard for me to imagine why anyone would consider competitiveness inherently harmful. I imagine this sentiment is held exclusively by those who don't know how to win. Losers hate competition. They're no good at it; they simply don't have what it takes to thrive in competitive environments. Rather than develop the skill set to succeed in a competitive environment, those with a loser mentality will complain that the game exists at all or that it is somehow rigged against them.

It's easy to tell who these individuals are. They'll say the metrics that determine success don't matter. For example, I've heard businessmen proudly proclaim, "Money isn't important to me." I call B.S. It may not be the *most* important metric to you, but to say that you're a businessman who isn't interested in building financial capital is disingenuous. These people also have a habit of downplaying the high performance of others. I often hear phrases like, "You're so lucky," as others perceive my relative success with the Order of Man movement. I'm not lucky! Sure, I've benefitted from things like being born in the United States of America, where, despite her flaws, we still believe the best way to unleash human ingenuity is to unlock and cultivate the personal incentive to perform.

103

Another dead giveaway is the phrase, "_____ isn't fair." Right, it's not fair. And? Life doesn't allow anyone to start in the same place. Sure, some have advantages others do not. Some also have disadvantages others do not. Does that mean the game doesn't exist? Does that mean those with competitive advantages ought to cripple themselves to allow others a chance? Of course not. Why would you hinder your own performance because others lack the ability to elevate theirs? When you do, not only do you hobble yourself, but you hobble others. You cannot help people up if you aren't in the position to do so. Cowering to make others feel comfortable is antithetical to building influence, credibility, and authority with them. Competitiveness, however, drives you to seek the position that serves others best.

Competitiveness drives innovation, ingenuity, creativity, skill development, efficiency, cost reduction, and opportunity. Apathy leads to mediocrity, complacency, ineffectiveness, and underperformance.

I'll admit that competitiveness taken to the extreme of winning at all costs can create a destructive environment and a less-than-favorable long-term outcome. But that isn't inherent to competition.

Complaining about competition, or that the game is somehow unfair, is rooted in victimhood. Those who complain about it often paint themselves as perpetual victims who are at the mercy of outside and unchangeable factors and circumstances. You aren't a victim. You may have been victimized, but choosing whether to remain in that state or to lift yourself out of it is something you have complete control over. You're going to need every ounce of your competitive nature and drive to do it.

There is also danger in buying into the idea that there is only a finite amount of success to go around and when one man pulls out ahead of another, he sucks up the limited resources available. That is a mindset of poverty.

When I was younger and infinitely more immature, I would often see people around me winning and consider it a direct threat to my own success. Sure, I'd give my friends who were succeeding the obligatory pat on the back, smile my fake smile, and congratulate them as I secretly despised the fact that they were succeeding when I wasn't. But what I've since learned is that the success of others does not hinder my own; instead, it paves the way for me to produce the type of result I'm after. The fact that others succeed makes it easier for me to win, not harder.

Dave Ramsey, author of the *New York Times* bestseller *The Total Money Makeover* and the founder of Financial Peace University and Ramsey Solutions, recently explained to me the concept of the "cake vs. candle mentality."

Those with a "cake" mentality look at life like a cake: there's only so much to go around. If there are ten people at a party, each person gets a tenth of the cake. If there are a hundred people at the party, each person gets a hundredth of the cake. Knowing this (and if you love cake), you can see why you'd want other people either to not show up or to decline their piece. The fewer people who partake, the more you get.

A candle on a cake is different. Once lit, the candle can then be used to light other candles. Lighting another candle does nothing to diminish the value of the previous candle. In fact, it only increases its worth, as it becomes a resource that adds value to the environment around it. Although the original candle will, at some point, run out of fuel, its legacy is carried on by the other candles it lit.

Life is not a zero-sum game. It's an infinite game filled with infinite opportunities and solutions to the world's most pressing challenges.

Competition, therefore, isn't a problem. It's a solution. Competition and the desire to win have created some of the most prosperous times the world has ever known.

If you can learn how to wield the power of competition to draw out the best in yourself and others, they'll always view you as a strong, powerful leader capable of maximizing personal performance. And who doesn't want the best for themselves?

COMPETE WITH OTHERS, COMPETE WITH YOURSELF

In 2015, as I was starting the Order of Man movement and podcast, I spent a lot of time searching for the inspiration and direction I needed to get this movement off the ground. I was anxious to make my mark on the world and expected a lot of myself as I embarked on this new journey.

I found inspiration everywhere, including podcasts, blogs, websites, stores I shopped at, magazines, and even billboards I saw. One resource I had been following for quite some time was the Art of Manliness, founded by Brett McKay. I consumed everything I possibly could from Brett's site. I immersed myself in what he did, how often he released podcasts and blogs, his writing style, etc. Hell, I even researched the events and conferences he was attending.

The very first blog post I ever made on our website was "How to Throw a Baseball." Useful information, no doubt, but quite different than what you'd expect to see from the Order of Man so many have come to love today. As I write that, I can't help but think that headline sounds more like an Art of Manliness resource than an Order of Man one.

I became so consumed with what Art of Manliness was doing that I damn near lost my mind. I would get frustrated with our rate of growth relative to theirs and ask myself why we weren't producing the same results they were seeing. I would throw pity parties for myself and feel completely deflated by our lack of growth relative to what Brett and others were experiencing.

Then, one day, in the midst of a particularly pathetic wallow session, I made a decision to unfollow *all* Art of Manliness social media channels; unsubscribe from receiving its videos, emails, and resources; and stop reading/engaging with any of its content.

It was instantaneously liberating. I had been so immersed in comparing myself to the "competition" that it became debilitating to my own progress. That's actually one of the problems with competition. We often find ways to beat ourselves up by comparing our beginning to someone else's middle or end. Or, in the case of social media, we compare our "lowlight reel" to somebody else's highlight reel.

I've since started following Art of Manliness again, but I'm in a completely different, much healthier space than I was when I launched this thing years ago. I no longer feel the need to compare my site to what others are doing. That's not to say I don't *observe* what they're doing, but I only do so as an opportunity to learn from their success, not deflate myself because of it.

Take, for example, another person I follow (who happens to be a good friend and mentor), Sean Whalen. If you're not familiar with Sean, he is the founder and owner of Lions Not Sheep (among many other businesses). From the outside looking in, you might consider us competitors. I don't. I consider him inspiration. I don't have to compete with Sean in order to win, and he doesn't have to compete with me to do the same. As of November 2021, there were an estimated 7.9 billion people on the planet. There are plenty of customers/clients/listeners/ etc. to go around.

Outside of sports or hypercompetitive business environments, there isn't really any need to compare yourself to other people and let it become a referendum on you. Comparison doesn't help you win, but only deters you from doing so.

That said, there is *someone* you should compare yourself to: the man you were yesterday. That's it. If you can show up and perform better than you did yesterday, you win. Period. End of story.

So many of us are directing our competitive energy toward nonproductive outlets and factors outside our control. I can't control what Brett or Sean do, *but* I can control what I do. And that's exactly where we should place the emphasis for ourselves and those under our care.

Your goal should be to compete with the man you used to be, even if only twelve hours ago. And you ought to pay attention to those you wish to lead to ensure they're doing the same. It's never served anyone to take external competition to the extreme—and in many ways, you're only placing a governor on the well-being of yourself, your family, and your team when you do.

With all that said, there is *some* value to be found in comparing yourself to what others in your market are doing, whether it's a business model you're inspired by, a father who is leading his family well, or the man at the gym who seems to have developed the discipline you desire.

If what others are doing is paving the path, why in the world would we not look to those individuals to highlight what is possible for us? That can become a source of influence, motivation, and guidance on your own path to self-development. It's not the "comparison trap" too many men fall into.

One question I often get regarding my podcast goes something like this: "Ryan, I really enjoy listening to your high-profile guests, but can you please interview a 'regular guy'?"

Why would I do that? Why would I use such a powerful platform to interview someone who hasn't yet made it to a place you or I are trying to go? Why would anyone even ask me to in the first place? Well, the answer is simple. Anyone who asks this question typically has a difficult time relating to some of these hard-charging high performers. Good! That's the point. If you related with them all, you really wouldn't have much need to learn from them. You're not supposed to relate to them. What you're supposed to do is learn from and emulate their actions so that you can replicate in your own life the results they've been able to produce.

You're not supposed to be comfortable with where you are. Comfort breeds complacency. And complacency gets you destroyed. If you want to talk with a regular guy, go talk with your neighbor at the community barbecue you're hosting this weekend. If you want to win (and help others do the same), look for the best of the best—not to compare yourself to them, but to give you a clear path for unlocking all the potential that lies dormant within you.

STACK THE DECK

Competition frightens so many people that we do everything we can to avoid it. If you have children, consider your local recreational sports league. I've coached youth sports for a long time, and I'm amazed and repulsed by how often the rules explicitly eliminate keeping score. "Well, ummm, like, uhhh, we just want to the kids to focus on learning the game and getting better," the proponents stutter.

Yeah, I understand that. That's the entire point of competitive sports. But what better way to teach them than to give them a benchmark for their performance? "But, Ryan," they'll plead with me, "there are more important things than winning."

"Yeah, like what?" I'll retort. They usually cite myriad virtues, like honor, integrity, hard work, discipline, etc., etc., etc. While I agree with all that, I've never once had anyone willing and able to explain to me how keeping score is at odds with any of those virtues. In fact, those very virtues are what lead to winning in the first place.

Think about it. Are you going to stand there, look me in the eye, and sincerely suggest that you aren't interested in winning the attention of a beautiful woman, the admiration of your children, that promotion at work, the large client you and another company are fighting for, and countless other ambitions you have?

Yes, the way you win is important. We've already discussed that in this book, and I went into depth on it in my first book, *Sovereignty*. Honor matters. Integrity matters. Self-respect matters (more on that in Chapter 15). But so does winning.

So much so that you have a moral obligation to win and help your team (family, friends, neighbors, employees, coworkers, etc.) do the same. And if that's the goal, you need to find a way to give yourself the best chance of doing so.

We started this chapter by talking about perceived and actual advantages and disadvantages people have in life. No one can deny that some individuals are better at certain things than others are. I, for example, am extremely good at fixating on a target and going after it relentlessly until I achieve my objective. I am not good, however, at the day-to-day details of ensuring my plans work with maximum efficiency.

Your job as a leader is to look for and capitalize on the advantages you and your team possess and to minimize weaknesses. If you have an analytical person on your team who enjoys endlessly combing through numbers, looking for inefficiencies in the finance department, it may not be the best call to place him on the marketing team to interact with and secure potential new clients. That probably just doesn't make sense. But it would make sense to have him work with the marketing department to measure the ROI on ads, direct mail, and other marketing strategies.

See, we spend so much time comparing ourselves to others and believing that we need to do it exactly the way everyone else does it that we often overlook our own unique advantages or how to best utilize the people we're responsible for. Take my last example. Not only does it make sense to do that from a business perspective, but the employee who is given the freedom to pursue his or her unique talents, gifts, and abilities will work harder for the cause.

This is what I call "stacking the deck." For example, I may not be as connected as other people in the business are. I may not have the same level of wealth some do. I may not have a certain skill or talent that others inherently possess. But I don't dwell on that. And I certainly don't paint myself as a victim because of it.

Instead, I spend time tapping into the gifts, talents, abilities, resources, and opportunities that I do possess to make up for my deficiencies in other areas. As I do, I learn to become resilient and creative and often find new ways to utilize existing technology and information. It's also a powerful way to unleash the potential in others. There is no one as valuable in the eyes of those you wish to lead than someone who empowers them to do something they love and gives them the tools to maximize it.

Don't ever fall into the trap of believing that competition is bad. And don't ever cripple yourself or your people so that others can keep up. It might make some feel better about their lagging performance, but what are you doing to your own psyche and well-being and those who could otherwise be served by a leader who wants to win and helps his people tap into everything they have to do so?

TRAPS AND TACTICS

Competition is one of the greatest factors a man can tap into when it comes to improving himself, his environment, and those around him.

Sure, a man can take it to the extreme and fall into the trap of competing solely for the sake of competition. If he does, winning becomes the only thing that matters and oftentimes, he will be more likely to jeopardize morals and values just for the sake of winning. The ends do not justify the means.

But using your desire to compete in constructive ways leads to positive results. A man should not shy away from his competitive nature but instead look for ways to use it as the fuel for growth and expansion in his life.

Measure Everything You Want to Improve

The first step to improvement always starts with measuring your current performance. In many ways, this can be one of the most challenging aspects of growth. We spend so much time, even subconsciously, deluding ourselves into thinking that we're performing much better than we actually are. There is only one way to get to the truth of the matter: measure your performance objectively.

If you want to lose weight, get on the scale. If you want to build wealth, look at your bank account. If you want to pay off debt, pull out the credit card statements. If you know you should do this and haven't, it's time. Make the decision today to take a good, long look at reality so you can actually do something about it.

Once you do, turn your plan into a game. If you're $53,000 in debt today, make it a goal to be $52,000 in debt by the end of the month. If you're fifty pounds overweight, make it a goal to be forty-five pounds overweight in thirty days.

Turn that competitive drive into a competition with the weaker, lazier, more pathetic version of yourself . . . and win! It starts with knowing where you stand and what the score currently is.

Double Down on Strengths

You are exceptionally good at a few things, and you're exceptionally bad at others. So many men dwell on what they aren't that they often overlook what they are. Take some time to explore who and what you are and what you're really, really good at doing in your life. And capitalize on it.

Are you a great networker? Do you have a specific set of skills that would make you valuable to an organization? Do you enjoy tinkering with mechanics? Are you good with technology? Are you a great researcher? Are you a great salesman?

As you begin to explore where you're talented, gifted, and skilled, don't shirk from using every advantage you have to your benefit. Yes, others will complain that a certain connection, resource, or skill set you possess tips the balance of the competition in your favor. And? That's something only losers complain about. While they could be figuring out how to maximize their strengths, they're too busy sitting on the sidelines, whining about what everyone else is doing.

Besides, if you want to create a winning environment for yourself and others, you're going to have to know more about yourself and your team than you currently do. Armed with that knowledge and ensuring all the players are in the right position not only helps you win, but it empowers your team to make the most of themselves. You should be the one to do it.

Mind Your Business

When I was playing competitive sports in high school, my teammates and I would often complain that a referee made a bad call. We'd conveniently pin a loss on him and his inability to call the game correctly and/or fairly.

Our coach would frequently remind us that the game should never be so close that one bad referee or even one bad call could determine the outcome. He taught us to put the responsibility where it lay: on our shoulders. In spite of outside circumstances beyond our control, it was our responsibility to focus on the things we could control so that the outside factors became less relevant.

Many men never grow out of that, and instead of focusing on their own performance, they spend an insane amount of time explaining how, if only a few outside factors had been different, their performance would have been elevated.

You've got to get over that mentality. It serves no one to focus on what others are doing at the expense of what you are. This is why I always suggest to men that they mind their own business. Break down your performance. If you fell short, ask yourself what you personally could have done to improve. Then, make your moves.

Besides, if you're spending time focused on what the other team is doing (or factors beyond your control), you're either going to feel deflated and inferior or you're going to let your pride take over because you think you're superior. Either outcome leads to weak planning, less practice, and poor performance.

Your ability to mind your business is the most powerful tool in your arsenal.

Analyze, Don't Critique

It's easy to look at what another person is doing and simply write it off as "luck." Another strategy I've seen men use to make themselves feel better about who they are is to attribute another man's success to malicious actions. "The only reason that guy is successful is because he cheated his way to get there," I'll often hear men say. They'll accuse someone of lying, stealing, and exploiting others to get to the top. While there is certainly some of that going on, in my experience, the most successful men I've interacted with simply add more value than average men do. Period.

So, if you're going to spend any amount of time focusing on what other people do (and there is value in that), you might as well be spending that time focused on productive behaviors. Crying about why "life is unfair," "the rich get richer," and "some guys have all the luck" is doing nothing to move the needle in your own life.

Instead of resenting others' success, learn to analyze the behavior that got them there in the first place. As is often said, "Success leaves clues." That is true, but you have to look for them, and you have to be willing to apply them. Learning to shut up, listen, observe, and act has paid huge dividends in my life. Complaining about someone else never has.

CHAPTER TEN

DOMINANCE

*I don't just want to go out there and do my job—I want
to excel at it. I hold myself to a high standard. I expect
to make plays that alter the game, and if I don't, I hold
myself accountable.*

—Clay Matthews III

The word *dominate* comes from the Latin word *dominari,* which
means "to rule or to govern." But viewed in the popular narrative,
dominance has less to do with the skill and aptitude of individuals or
teams and more to do with unrighteous control over others. That isn't
dominance, that's abuse.

There isn't a chance in hell that any sort of abuse leads to influence,
authority, and credibility with others. You might be able to abuse someone
mentally, physically, and/or emotionally to garner their compliance, but it
won't earn you their commitment (see Chapter Three).

Besides, dominance isn't really about others, anyway. Dominance
is about doing what you need to do to develop your skills and talents
in a way that serves you and your team most effectively. Sure, there may
be others who will be negatively impacted by your ability to dominate,
for example, on the Jiu-Jitsu mats or in the boardroom, but that is an
inevitable outcome of your discipline and dedication. In order to win,
you're going to have to learn how to dominate any space in which you
find yourself.

I often think back to my time in service when it comes to dominance. I joined the Utah Army National Guard when I was a senior in high school, and in 2005, I found myself in Ramadi, Iraq, one of the most dangerous locations at the time in all of the Iraq War.

We worked for six months to prepare ourselves for that twelve-month tour. Our training consisted entirely of developing maximum proficiency with the weapons, tools, and resources we had at our disposal. Never once did we train to be less effective or efficient than we could otherwise be. We had a job to do: serve the people of Iraq and destroy our enemies. That's always been the objective of any military unit. It's obvious that destroying the enemy is the primary purpose of any fighting force. Or so you'd think.

Compare the objective of literally every military force that ever existed—fight and destroy—with today's military, where woke policy, gender theory, diversity training, and diminishing training requirements have infiltrated the list of top priorities. Our military is becoming less lethal because of it. There's a problem with that: people die needlessly.

I saw it firsthand. I am intimately familiar with what happens when a mission goes wrong or our military members lack the training and tools to complete their objective favorably.

Fortunately, most of society will never have to experience that for themselves. I'm grateful for that, but let's not pretend that the same lesson (to a lesser degree) hasn't permeated much of the rest of society.

What would happen if you did not train to become proficient in your job? You'd get fired. What would happen if you shirked your responsibilities at home and ghosted your family, put other priorities above them, and made them feel unimportant? You'd lose them. What would happen if you let your body go, ate like crap all the time, and never worked out a day in your life? You'd get fat and run into health complications.

The consequences for living your life passively are not unknown. We know exactly what would happen in the above examples and others, yet we still engage in the behaviors that lead to a place of mediocrity and unmet potential.

Instead, I'd encourage us all to dominate in any environment we find ourselves. Isn't that the point—to become the best we can possibly be?

If you're going to spend time at work, be the best employee the company has ever had. If you're going to have a conversation with your wife after work, make it the most engaged and meaningful conversation you two have ever had. If you're going to go to the gym and train for an hour, make it the most effective and efficient hour spent. If you're going to start a podcast or business, do everything you can to leverage all the tools available and be the best.

Often, when I share advice like this, I'm met with hesitancy. "Ryan, I don't have to be the best at everything. Sometimes I just want to do things to enjoy them," men will say. I agree with that sentiment. As I shared in the previous chapter, competition is not always about beating someone else. Sometimes it's about beating the man you were yesterday. If that means you enjoy painting, working on cars, hunting, composing music, reading good books, training Jiu-Jitsu, etc., as a hobby, you can and will find joy in being the best you can be, not necessarily besting someone else.

POWER DYNAMICS VERSUS APTITUDE DYNAMICS

I'm amazed how often I hear others complain that the only reason one man got ahead is because he did so at another's expense. I know this happens, but I'd suggest that's the exception, not the rule. Power gained at the expense of others is usually short-lived. Once those he wishes to subjugate discover who he truly is, they rise up and rebel against the tyrant.

Conversely, men who understand that true and lasting influence, credibility, and authority come from making the most of their time on this spinning rock and helping other people do the same are men who truly change the world for the better.

But that lasting change is a function of aptitude, not simply the quest for power. Interestingly enough, when you learn to develop a set of skills that serves you and others well, you *are* granted more power in all of its forms. That is the inevitable result.

Is power something to be shunned? I would argue that it's not. What good can you possibly do without the money, influence, notoriety, tools, and resources that are derived from power? What good does it do to those you care about to play small because you're afraid to be powerful?

Seven years ago, I was a know-nothing guy who wanted to start a podcast. I owned a financial planning practice that was doing well, but I was looking for something more in my life. I had always felt like there was something calling to me and that I was destined (for lack of a better term) to serve others in a way I hadn't been serving them previously. I was paying the bills and providing for my family, but it didn't seem to quench my thirst for making a real difference in the world.

I stumbled and fumbled my way through my early podcasting career. After about three years, I began to feel like I was finding my stride. Now, after seven years of podcasting, I can confidently say that the notoriety I've earned is infinitely better than what I had when I started out.

Consider this: with a podcast that has been downloaded over forty-five million times and all the attention that comes with it, I'm in an incredibly wonderful position to serve as many people as possible. I couldn't say the same when we were reaching a hundred or even a thousand people.

Working to develop power in your life is not inherently negative. How many people could you feed if you made $400,000 a year as opposed to $40,000? How many lives could you impact if you employed five hundred people instead of five? How much time, attention, and energy could you devote to your family, friends, and community if you were fully able to tap into the potential that exists inside you?

My friend, Bedros Keuilian, the founder of Fit Body Boot Camp, MDK Project, Squire Program, and coach to some of the most notable entrepreneurs on the planet, has used his much-deserved wealth and abundance to serve others. To date, he has donated more than $1.2 million to Shriners Hospitals for Children and $600,000 to Toys for Tots, and he's sponsored ninety-seven children through Compassion International. Bedros immigrated to America with his family when he was six years old. He once told me that, when he was young, his family was so destitute that his parents siphoned gas out of a vehicle on the street to kill his head lice. In spite of that beginning, Bedros has gone on to become a wildly successful entrepreneur and build an empire that has directly and positively impacted millions of people across the planet. Do you believe for one second that he is an individual who is not interested in dominating every facet of his life? Again, not for his own personal gain, but in service to others.

Here is another way to look at it. How many people are you *not* serving because you're playing it safe? How many lives could you impact if you decided that you were going to dominate your life, not at the *expense* of others but *for* them?

I believe the real question is, which is more dangerous to you, your loved ones, and society as a whole: you surrendering who you have the potential to become, or you dominating every single aspect of your life so that you may serve as many people as possible?

But here's the deal: You don't get to skip the power line. You don't get to have the influence, authority, and credibility you desire simply because you want it. You have to *earn* it. That's what I learned in the first few years of podcasting, and that's what Bedros has learned over decades of building his organizations. In the early days, I would reach out to potential podcast guests and get rejected or ghosted altogether. I would hear a lot of doubt in people's voices when I shared my opinions. It felt like I was pulling teeth, trying to get people to pay attention to what I had to say. Frankly, I had a false expectation about how long it would take to develop the trust I wanted from others.

So, I went to work. I worked on my podcasting skills. I listened to as many podcasts as I possibly could and paid attention to how good interviewers conducted their shows. I started to invest in new equipment. I experimented with the emails I was sending to potential guests. I did all of this and more. And, slowly and gradually, I began to notice that what I was saying was beginning to carry more weight with those who would listen.

It's been a long road, and we still have so much further to travel, but I understand now that if I truly want to become a powerful individual (not just for myself but for others), it's a painstaking process of developing the skill, talents, and aptitude for success.

You can do this too, but you can't be afraid of power. There is nothing inherently wrong with power and dominating your field to acquire it. I'm reminded of a verse in the Bible, 1 Timothy 6:10 (KJV): "For the love of money is the root of all evil: which while some coveted after, they have erred from faith, and pierced themselves through with many sorrows."

Too many people interpret that passage to mean that *money* is inherently evil, but if you pay close attention to the actual words used, you'll notice it says "the *love* of money is the root of all evil."

The same can be said of power. If you're after power for the sake of power, you're playing a dangerous game—one that will drive you to risk your personal morals and principles. If, however, you want to use the power you wield (or could wield) to lift others up, go *dominate* and earn it.

EXPECT THE BEST OF YOURSELF

It does no good to play small. It really doesn't. Society doesn't expect much of you. If you make poor financial decisions, just declare bankruptcy. If your marriage gets a little challenging, just file for divorce. If you prove yourself incompetent and get fired from your job, no problem, claim unemployment benefits. Can that really be the answer to what ails us—to build in a bunch of safety nets to rescue people from bad decisions?

I don't believe so, because it promotes mediocrity. Mediocrity, though, is the antithesis to what is required if you hope to establish influence, credibility, and authority with others along your path. Instead, you ought to fully embrace who you have the potential to become. You ought to be empowering that in others as well.

I've got a friend here in Maine whose oldest son is extremely tall for his age. Whenever my friend goes to one of his games, he brings his son's birth certificate with him because he knows, without question, the other team is going to ask him to prove that his son is, in fact, eligible to play in the league.

My friend's son's own coach has benched him and asked him not to play to his full potential "because it isn't fair." What a shame. What a shame that we are conditioning our children from such an early age to do less than they're capable of. What lesson are you teaching your people (and yourself) when you don't give your very best effort?

I can't imagine the look on that young man's face when he is benched by his coach, someone who is supposed to be an advocate for him to help him reach his full potential. I can't imagine how that translates to other facets of this young man's life.

I reject the idea that you should do less than you can because someone is incapable or unwilling to keep up.

One of my early mentors in my budding financial planning practice used to say, "Ryan, you will be successful when you learn to light yourself on fire and allow others to watch you burn." I really didn't know what he meant at the time. I was struggling then to build my financial planning practice from the ground up. I knew I had talent, but not only did I not know what I needed to be doing, I was afraid of others' judgment. So I played it safe. I tried not to ruffle any feathers, and instead, I worked to blend into the crowd—never the worst performer but never the best.

It wasn't until my mentor told me to light myself on fire that, for the first time in my life, I really began to go all in on my business and myself. What an incredible difference that made, not only in myself but in those around me.

It's been said that "a rising tide lifts all ships." Truer words have never been spoken, especially as it relates to developing the influence, authority, and credibility you desire and the fulfillment that comes with it.

Your team's ability correlates directly to yours, and if you are either limiting your own performance or hindering theirs out of some false sense of fear that they may begin to outperform you, you are no leader at all.

Demand the very best of yourself. Expect the very best of your team. When they fall short, empower them with the time, attention, resources, energy, and tools they need to play at 100 percent.

Inside our exclusive brotherhood, the Iron Council, more than fifteen hundred men are working together to become more than we currently are. Admittedly, there are those who are infinitely more skilled in certain aspects of their lives than I currently am. I can be intimidated by that, or I can empower them to elevate my own performance and the performance of others inside the Council. How selfish does one man need to be to hamstring another man's performance because he's intimidated by it? Instead, we ought to be looking for ways to elevate the performance of others. That doesn't make you "less than." If anything, it gives you the opportunity to improve and increase your own performance.

Men don't play small. They don't ask others to play small. If they're worried someone is better than them, good—it gives a man an opportunity for growth. We don't wallow in our inadequacies; we do what is necessary to grow, thrive, and dominate. And we give our people all the tools and resources they need to do the same in their lives.

Winners beget winners. Losers beget losers. If you find yourself looking around your sphere of influence and wondering why they're not performing, take a good look at yourself and ask why you're not performing. Then do something about it, for your sake and the sake of your team.

TRAPS AND TACTICS

My friend Andy Frisella, founder of 1st Phorm and the host of the *Real AF* podcast, often talks about what he describes as the 100–0 mentality. Yes, it's a sports reference (meaning the score is 100–0), but it applies equally to every facet of our lives. Don't ever believe that righteousness comes in playing small or holding yourself back. In fact, I would suggest that it is *unrighteous* to play to a degree less than you're capable of.

Understand also that those under your care want to play for a winning team. No person ever wanted to play on the losing side of the equation. If you can learn to dominate in all areas of your life, and help others do the same, you have the power to make yourself indispensable.

Get Good at Saying No, and Become Obsessed

You can do anything you want to do, but you can't possibly do everything. It's a lesson I've had to learn the hard way through a lot of trial and error. I used to try to do it all. I would say yes to every request and opportunity that came my way. While I was trying to be helpful to others and myself, I realized that instead of being proficient and effective at everything, I became so-so at a lot of things.

There is no possible way to dominate in every area of your life. Instead, I recommend nailing down where exactly you want to dominate. I, for example, want to create one of the largest podcasts on the planet. That said, I don't want to edit the largest podcast, I want to host it. So I hire out aspects of the podcast that need to get done: editing, uploading, promotion, marketing, etc. This allows me to focus on very specific skills that will make me the best and, simultaneously, allows others to do the same in their respective fields.

Know what you want. Know what you don't want. Commit to being the best at what you're after. Give others an opportunity to do the same with what they're after.

Practice the Skills of High Performers

These days, there is no excuse not to know how to do something. The only reason you don't is because you either don't want it bad enough or you're just getting started. If you're just getting started, that's understandable. You're on the path. If, however, you're telling yourself you want something but you're unwilling to put in the work to have it, that's unacceptable.

Between podcasts, YouTube, online courses, in-person events, books, etc., there is simply no reason not to dominate in any environment. Once you've identified where you want to dominate, dedicate time *every single day* to mastering the craft.

If you want to play the guitar, play the guitar. If you want to run a marathon, run. If you want to write a book, write (I personally wrote no fewer than a thousand words per day on average to complete this book). If you want to get good at martial arts, train. That's it. It's that simple. Learn not to take so much pride in the results you and others produce, and, instead, reward consistency toward the desired outcome. If you find and recognize value in your own personal journey and the journey of others, you'll eventually dominate your field, without question.

Don't Base Performance on How You Feel

As I write this chapter today, I'm feeling a bit under the weather—just a mild, seasonal head cold. Truth be told, I'd rather be lying in bed milking this cold for all it's worth, but I'm not. I'm up and writing precisely because I said I would. That's what's required.

In 1997, Michael Jordan played in his infamous "Flu Game." It wasn't the flu—he had suffered food poisoning the night before. Regardless, he got up and played. He ended up scoring thirty-eight points and hitting the game-winning three-pointer that gave the Bulls a 3–2 lead over the Jazz in Game Five of the NBA Finals.

These types of stories aren't uncommon in those who dominate their fields. The best of the best perform regardless of how they feel in any given scenario. That's why they're the best—they do what is required to win and dominate.

Whether you're dealing with a physical illness, an emotional or mental hardship, or you just "don't feel like it," do it anyway. That's what's required. If everyone performed only when they were 100 percent, the world would look much different than it does today. Show up day in and day out, whether you feel like it or not.

Surround Yourself with Producers

In my forty years on this spinning rock, I've come to realize, as I shared earlier, that there are only two types of people: those who consume more than they produce (consumers) and those who produce more than they consume (producers).

Producers are a different breed. Where consumers see problems, producers see solutions. Where consumers see obstacles, producers see opportunity. Where consumers are skeptical of others and life in general, producers are optimistic in their outlook.

Producers are the kind of people you want to surround yourself with. They don't put up with bullshit. They don't tolerate underperformance. And they don't allow others to perform to a degree less than they're capable of. If you ever find yourself around people who discount your effort, mock you for going above and beyond, or laugh because "you're trying too hard," you know you're around consumers.

If, on the other hand, you find yourself around those who celebrate your success, don't tolerate inadequacy and empower you to do more, and support you in your dreams and desires, congrats—you're around producers.

Be very deliberate and intentional about who you surround yourself with. Those people will contribute greatly to whether you slink away into mediocrity or perform at the highest level you possibly can.

CHAPTER ELEVEN

AGGRESSION

Obstacles don't have to stop you. If you run into a wall, don't turn around and give up. Figure out how to climb it, go through it, or work around it.

—*Michael Jordan*

Before we get into the topic of aggression, let's talk about why it's so important that we do. In modern society, we seem to have become so averse to the concept of aggression that even the word intimidates and scares people. At the slightest hint of what some may consider aggressive behavior (calling someone a bad name, "misgendering" a person, using a swear word, or simply holding a different opinion about a polarizing subject), they may be accused of committing "microaggressions" against another.

We mock the "wokesters" who perpetuate this nonsense, but make no mistake, many men have bought into the idea that aggression is inherently destructive or "harmful" (as the APA puts it). How do I know this? Because every week I hear from hundreds of men who call themselves "recovering nice guys."

These are men who, for years, have allowed themselves to be trampled on and railroaded by their bosses, colleagues, coworkers, wives, girlfriends, and everyone else in their lives. They know they want to assert themselves but they either A) don't know how or B) are afraid that others might consider them to be assholes (we'll revisit this in a bit).

I know from experience what it's like to be a "nice guy." ("Nice" is not to be confused with "kind.") For years, I did everything I was "supposed" to do, always looking for a pat on the head from the person whose approval I sought most. I thought the best way to get what I wanted was to be civil. And, to a certain degree, civility is required, but not at the expense of our own sanity, well-being, and masculine nature.

Jordan Peterson, author of *12 Rules for Life* and *Beyond Order*, often makes the case against being too agreeable. What's wrong with being agreeable? Nothing, as long as you can rein it in. But taken to the extreme, agreeableness keeps you from going after what you want. Peterson says of the thousands of patients he's worked with, "Agreeable people do not like conflict."[1]

And if you don't like conflict, you might be more likely to sacrifice your own worthy ambitions for others. Conflict is inherent in progress, and it cannot be avoided if you hope to achieve lofty ambitions.

Over-agreeableness turns men into spineless cowards who will do and say anything to avoid confrontation or make themselves look too aggressive in others' eyes.

Years ago, I had a business partner who was so afraid of confrontation that it eventually drove a wedge into our friendship and business. In turn, there was a lot of tension and animosity between us.

He didn't like the way I handled portions of the business, but instead of discussing it with me, he refused to even broach the subject. I noticed his contention growing, but each time I suggested we talk about it, he deflected. It wasn't that he didn't hold any negative feelings toward me. It was that he was unable or unwilling to share them. He was afraid, and because he lacked the ability to discuss these aspects of the business, we eventually ended up dissolving it—costing us both plenty of time and plenty of money.

I'm fairly certain that you've either had a similar experience with someone that passive, or perhaps you are that person. Either way, it creates problems that don't need to exist . . . if you can learn to be comfortable with confrontation.

Equally troubling (maybe even more so) is that much of society perpetuates the sedation, emasculation, and domestication of men.

Strong, bold men who know what they want are a threat to the powers that be. These men (the type you likely have a desire to become) are much more difficult to control. So we're often presented with "studies" from the APA and other medical associations that preach the dangers of masculinity; we're met with phrases like "toxic masculinity," "rape culture," and "tyrannical patriarchy," designed to paint all masculinity as dangerous and subdue otherwise ambitious men. In the entertainment industry, men are often portrayed as bumbling idiots incapable of tying their own shoes, let alone leading others well.

So, why is aggression so important? Because the alternative is unacceptable. The alternative is a society of pathetic wimps willing to roll over on their own and others' dreams in exchange for safety and comfort, and millions of people living lives that are inferior to what they otherwise could be.

Don't you have dreams? Don't you have desires? Do you care so little about yourself and others that you're willing to live as a shell of the man you have the potential to become?

Don't get it wrong: aggressive doesn't mean dangerous. You can be aggressive and be an asset to yourself and others, not a liability. In fact, learning how to tap into and harness your aggression for productive outcomes makes you more of an asset, not less.

AGGRESSIVE DOES NOT EQUAL RECKLESS

As you're reading this, you might be tempted to believe that one doesn't need to be aggressive to overcome the passivity that is plaguing society. That derives from a sense that aggression is limited to physical rage and recklessness. It isn't. Aggressive doesn't mean dangerous. It doesn't give anyone a license to hurt others physically, mentally, and/or emotionally.

Used correctly, aggression *can* absolutely serve you and others. And those leaders who aggressively go after their desires and help others do the same will always be looked upon more favorably than those who don't. As I mentioned earlier, if most people are afraid to go after what they want, the leader who actually does will win the influence, authority, and credibility of those who refuse to do it for themselves.

Over the past ten years (since my children started playing sports), I've coached dozens of youth baseball, football, and basketball teams. There is a clear and distinct performance difference between those children who are aggressive in their play and those who are not. The players who are aggressive hit the ball more often, score more often, force more errors from the other team, and generally outpace passive children in both athletic ability, physical performance, confidence, and success.

Do you believe this is any different for men? Of course it isn't. Those men who know exactly what they want and are unafraid to aggressively pursue it will likely achieve their ambitions significantly more than those who sit passively by, waiting for things to happen to them.

Unfortunately, too many men believe that their chances of success rely on some mystical force reserved only for the select few. I know. I used to believe that, too. I would look around at the men I envied, but instead of being motivated, I would get demoralized as I wondered when *I* would get as "lucky" as they were.

I *thought* I was being diligent in my pursuits, but I wasn't. Not even close. I would spend my days pretending to be working. I'd read dozens and dozens of books and not apply any of what I learned. I would research how to make sales calls, how to start a podcast, how to be successful in business. I read article after how-to article. And I had the audacity to believe I too could be a success? I wasn't doing any work. I was passively letting opportunities pass me by as I deluded myself into believing that I was putting in any real effort.

It wasn't until I learned to aggressively go after what I wanted that I stopped feeling sorry about my underperformance and gave myself a fighting chance to obtain what I wanted most out of life. You know, it's strange. I never had any problem with aggression as I played sports or, even now, as I train Jiu-Jitsu. For many men, it seems to come naturally in physical competition, but it's more difficult to translate into other facets of their lives.

I often wonder why we'll fight so hard on the basketball court with our buddies but refuse to bring the same level of intensity to our personal and professional goals. Consider how many people (your friends, family, clients, neighbors, etc.) would be served if you were more willing to exert the same level of fire toward your goals off the court or field.

Besides, you're going to need to tap into that aggression if you have any hope of leading yourself and others successfully through the obstacles of life. My high school football coach used to scold, "If you're going to make a mistake, do it at a hundred percent!" He was right. A hundred percent is what's required.

The next time you're tempted to ease up, pull back, and coast—don't! Use the masculine fire inside you to propel yourself through the challenging times—disease, bankruptcy, lawsuits, divorce, job layoffs, the reaction to a global pandemic, potentially losing your kids in a nasty custody battle, or anything else.

You deserve your best. Your people deserve your best. Don't fail them by buying into the idea that aggression is dangerous. It can be, if it's reckless. But you're not reckless, you're stoic (see Chapter Eight), and you know how to use every characteristic of who you are to benefit you and yours.

HOW INDIFFERENCE CAN SERVE YOU

I've found that most of the men I work with on a daily basis (even myself) who consider themselves to be "recovering nice guys" have an unhealthy relationship with what people think about them. Everything they do is predicated on the acceptance of others. Never mind the fact that what others think of you is largely outside your control. But the desire to fit in is such a driving force in men's lives that it often keeps them from prudent action and instead moves them into the realm of appeasing others and ensuring that everyone else feels okay with their decisions, actions, and performance.

So many men are walking on eggshells. Rather than risk the harsh judgment of others, they resign themselves to passivity and domestication.

In my first book *Sovereignty*, I talked at length about my separation from my wife. What I didn't get too much into detail on was the process of reconciliation after we had both made the decision to make the marriage work. When we reunited, I had a deep sense of fear that she would leave me again. I became consumed with ensuring that she knew I worshipped the ground she walked on. I tiptoed around every discussion and action. I felt I had given her a part of my soul, and it was pathetic. It was also extremely exhausting for me. I imagine it was equally exhausting for her. I wasn't her lapdog. And although her opinion counted (and still does), I realized that what she wanted and needed was a man who was decisive, bold, and assertive in leading her and our son well.

When we fear what others might think about us or what actions they might take as a result of that perception, we hinder our ability to perform at our highest level—aggressively.

Know this: *some* people's opinions matter (my wife's and my kids', for example), but not everyone's. You need to learn to let go of what other people think of you. It can be a real challenge because there is inherent risk in alienating yourself from others. But in today's climate, the risk is drastically reduced compared to what it might have been a hundred or a thousand years ago. You're not going to starve because some people don't like you. You're not going to be killed by a neighboring tribe because another person misinterpreted your aggressiveness and/or intensity as hate or hostility.

Look, you're going to be judged regardless of what you do. I know that I am every day. In fact, I'm almost inviting judgment every time I share my opinion on social media, the podcast, or even in this book. But with lots of practice and some thick skin, I've learned to let go of the opinions of others. When I cared more about what others think of me than I do now, I noticed myself hiding some of the fire within me.

What other people think of me is not my problem. I know there are plenty of individuals who can't handle masculine intensity. That's more of a referendum on them than it is on me. Many people read aggression as anger. It isn't. It's a metric of how much a person cares about a particular subject—*a* metric, not the *only* metric.

Again, many people can't handle it. But do you know who can? My family, friends, colleagues, clients, neighbors, etc., who are the beneficiaries of the fruit produced by a man who is sure enough of himself and what he wants that he's willing to pursue it relentlessly.

And, as a side benefit, when you care less about what others think of you, the more highly they will.

TRAPS AND TACTICS

Raw aggression scares people. They're intimidated by it. But they're also fascinated with it. We respect a man who aggressively pursues what he is after. We follow those types of men. No person on the planet is impressed with or inspired by someone who doesn't know what they want and/or isn't willing to do whatever is necessary to obtain it. Ask yourself whose team you would rather be on: the team that makes sure everyone feels comfortable with their poor performance or the team that gets you across the finish line. We all know the answer to this question. And we all know it takes aggression to get there.

Tiptoe into "Asshole Territory"

We talked earlier about recovering "nice guys." I am one, so I know how hard it is to pull yourself out of trying to please everyone who crosses your path. It's hard for nice guys to know the line, especially if they've never experimented with what is acceptable and what isn't. Don't misunderstand me. I'm not suggesting you go punch a random stranger or yell at your boss just so you can see how it goes. I am, however, asking you to take your assertiveness just a bit further than you feel comfortable with.

Here are a few exercises that will help:

- Say no to something you would normally say yes to and, for an added bonus, don't give the other person a reason. Just say no. And let that be it.
- When someone asks for your opinion, give it to them straight.
- For seven days, ask for a discount wherever you go to buy something—the restaurant, grocery store, movie theater, mall, etc. Just ask everywhere.

The point of these exercises is to make yourself uncomfortable and get you familiar with asserting yourself in a situation where you ordinarily would just want to slink away and hide. You can't know how to harness your aggression if you don't know where the line is. Be willing to cross it to find out.

Know EXACTLY What You Want

If I were to ask you right now, "What do you want out of life?" would you be able to tell me with precision? Or would you, like the majority of men, say something like, "I want to make a lot of money, have a good relationship, and feel good about myself"? That's boring, weak, and uninspiring. It's no wonder so many men aren't willing to get aggressive in their lives. There's nothing to get aggressive about.

Instead, what I'd like you to do is start getting crystal clear on what you want. More money? Great. How much more and in what time frame? Better relationship? Great. Does that mean more sex, conversations, connection, etc.? Tell yourself exactly what that means. Feel good about yourself? Okay, how do you quantify that? How will you know when you've achieved your objective?

Be precise. Be specific. Only then do you have the target to aggressively and relentlessly pursue.

Do More in the Next Three Months than You Did in the Last Twelve

Voluntary time constraints are an absolutely incredible thing. Parkinson's Law states that "work expands to fill the time allotted." So, if you have twelve months to accomplish a task, it will take you twelve months to accomplish it. If you have three months to accomplish the same task, you'll likely finish within that three-month window.

Now that you know what you want (if you did the last exercise), I want you to take your annual goals for the year and make them your quarterly goals. "Oh, but Ryan, that's impossible." Maybe it is. Maybe it isn't. You won't know unless you try it. And let's just assume I'm wrong. If I'm wrong, maybe it takes you six months instead of three. You still did it in half the time you were previously going to do it in. Not a bad downside.

If you shorten your time horizon, you'll have to develop your aggressiveness in your pursuit.

Eliminate Your Excuses and Stop Apologizing

We, as humans, are very good at justifying and excusing away our behavior. It's in our nature to do so. Heaven forbid we accept our own beliefs, ideals, and actions. It's a whole lot easier when we do, but often, we end up selling ourselves short because of it. We work tirelessly to appease others, and we become consumed with the way other people are feeling despite our own desires to relentlessly pursue what we're after.

Embrace the fact that you are an aggressive man, or at least you have the potential to become one. Yeah, there will be those who can't handle your focus, drive, determination, and relentlessness, but your goal isn't to appease the masses. Your goal is to lead yourself and others well, and those who could be led by you will appreciate your unwavering tenacity in doing it well.

Be aggressive. Own the fact that you are. And stop apologizing for embracing who you are. You don't owe anyone an apology. You owe it to yourself and others to harness the power of aggression to lead them to a place passive men simply cannot.

CHAPTER TWELVE

VIGILANCE

The condition upon which God hath given liberty to man is eternal vigilance.

—*John Philpot Curran*

One evening last year, after my wife and I tucked our four children into bed, I made my normal rounds. I checked the five entrance points to our home, locked the doors that needed to be locked, ensured the exterior lights were on, and went to bed.

I was awakened by a chime at around 2:30 a.m. A little delirious from sleep, I popped up and asked my wife, "Was that the doorbell?"

"I think so," she whispered.

Immediately, I jumped out of bed, grabbed the Glock 17 on my nightstand, and went to work.

I told her to pull up the security cameras while I went to look outside from the windows of the second story, where our bedroom is. I saw nothing. I went back to the bedroom to see if my wife had pulled up the camera. She had. There was a man standing outside our front door. At this point, I could hear him trying to open it.

"Call the police," I directed her. She did. I grabbed our four-year-old German shepherd and sent him downstairs. He didn't alert but sat at the bottom of the stairs on the first floor. Strange, I thought. He definitely would have alerted if someone were at the door. I made my way back to the bedroom to take a look at the multiple security cameras we have set up around our home. Nothing.

I went to the second-story windows and proceeded to check every window from that story (which happens to give us a 360-degree view of the perimeter of our house). I saw a white sedan sitting at the end of our driveway.

At that point, a squad car arrived (I was pleasantly surprised by the speed of their response). The officer pulled behind the sedan, got out with his flashlight, hand on his firearm, and approached the vehicle. I couldn't see much through the dark from inside, but I remained ready with my firearm and dog at my side. The officer pulled the man out of his car and after a few minutes talking with him, began to administer a field sobriety test. Another squad car arrived, and after a few minutes of watching the man fail to perform a number of requests any sober man could complete, the second officer arrested the man and drove off.

The first police officer approached our house. I had my wife grab the dog, and I opened the door. He informed me that the man was belligerently drunk and thought our house was a church where he could sleep off his intoxication. Believe it or not, it's a credible story. Ours is a large white house across the street from the large white Baptist church. A tow truck arrived not long after and removed the man's vehicle from our driveway.

Fortunately, that evening, the potential threat was neutralized without incident. But that's not to say it couldn't have gone an entirely different way. It could have been quite possible that the man did enter our home and, had he had more nefarious intentions than sleeping off his intoxication, I may have found myself fighting for my life and the lives of my family members.

This perfectly encapsulates the purpose of vigilance on a man's part. Simply put, it is our job to keep careful watch for danger, difficulties, adversity, and challenges on behalf of those we desire to lead. My plan—and there was a very deliberate plan in place to deal with intruders (more on that soon)—worked flawlessly. And that's for good reason. I anticipated it. My family talked about it. We drilled it. I didn't expect it to happen, but I made sure my family and I were ready if it did.

In Chapter Two, I made the case that among other things, a man is to be a protector of himself, those he loves, and those who are incapable of protecting themselves.

In order to fill this role, a man has to be vigilant about the danger his people might face. Although not everyone will have to face a home intrusion or some other dangerous encounter, our ability to remain vigilant and prepare for the unfortunate circumstances of life is a must, and a man who proves himself capable of keeping careful watch over those he cares about will earn influence, authority, and credibility with them.

There are many other scenarios outside home defense where vigilance will serve you and those you care about best:

- Driving down the road in icy conditions
- Anticipating changes in the economy
- Dealing with a business competitor
- Addressing potential illness, disability, and death
- Dealing with an act of violence in public
- Protesting, looting, and rioting in cities

The list of potential dangers you and yours face is endless. Yes, it's your responsibility as the man to deal with them when they arise, but more importantly than that, it's your job to anticipate what could happen before it happens in the first place.

This is what it means to be vigilant—to anticipate and address the inevitabilities of life that put you and others at risk. A man who learns to do that makes himself an incredibly powerful and much-needed asset to himself, his family, his neighbors, and his community.

PREDICT THE FUTURE?

Have you ever been caught in the rain without an umbrella, had a flat tire without a spare, or been surprised by a job layoff or divorce? If you have, that's your fault. I know it sounds harsh, but who else is to blame for the predicament you found yourself in? You may not think it's fair, but as I mentioned in Chapter Four, "fair" has nothing to do with your success (or lack thereof) or the success of those you're leading.

As frankly as I can say it, it's your job to know what the threats are. And, unfortunately, threats exist everywhere and can happen at any time. Are you prepared for them? You'll find out soon enough.

When my wife and I moved our family from southern Utah to Maine in 2019, we knew that the move was going to present its fair share of challenges. Chief among them was dealing with the harsh New England winters—something neither of us had had to deal with in the past.

I asked friends and neighbors what we needed in order to be prepared for the winter. Over and over, I heard three things: a snowplow, an efficient heating system, and a generator. Done. Those were among the first three purchases we made when we arrived. I'm glad we did. The newly installed heating system came in handy immediately as the temperatures began to drop. All six of us really appreciated the heat those radiators put off during the cold winter days. The snowplow was put to use not long after, once we experienced our first snowstorm. The generator didn't come in handy until months later.

As the winter season was coming to an end, I began to get a little frustrated that we had spent all that money on something we didn't even use. My tune changed quickly when we were hit with a particularly brutal ice storm. Within half a day, power had been knocked out around the county, and without skipping a beat, the generator (which had been hooked up directly to our electrical panel at the suggestion of those we asked) kicked on. Three days later, it was still running as power had not yet been restored.

I'm not sure what we would have done without that generator. The heating system requires power. Our water pump requires power. My work requires power. And so do all the creature comforts we've become accustomed to.

Consider an entirely different situation during the cold streak and power outages in Texas in 2021. Millions of people went without power because they were inadequately prepared for what could happen. It may be easy to say, "How could we have known?" And, while I can certainly understand the sentiment, it does nothing to ensure you and your people are taken care of. And when shit hits the proverbial fan, ignorance doesn't get the job done.

On the bright side, you don't actually have to predict the future. It is impossible, after all. All you need is a little knowledge, humility, and the common sense to look around and ask those who may know more than you, then act.

Retired Air Force Colonel John Boyd gave us a great framework for doing just that. It's called the OODA Loop, which is an acronym for Observe, Orient, Decide, and Act.

Observe

Whenever you find yourself in a new, unfamiliar situation, first, before anything else, observe your surroundings, your environment, and what threats you could potentially face. It does not serve you or others to look at every situation you find yourself in with naïve optimism. It may be easier, but it won't keep you and others protected and thriving. This is where situational awareness comes into play. Do you know where the threats are likely to come from? Do you know what your competition might be doing to render your services and products obsolete? Do you know your own weaknesses and vulnerabilities?

Those who aren't willing to exercise vigilance may suggest these practices border on paranoia. I disagree. The more you practice the art of observation, the more effective and proficient you become and the less time, resources, and energy it takes. Regardless, I'd rather be prepared and slightly paranoid than get caught with my pants down.

Orient

Now that you've observed your surroundings, whether at home, work, or out in the community, it's time to orient yourself relative to the potential threats. This is what I did when we moved to Maine and I asked others what I needed to ensure my family was safe during the winter. I knew our threats: blizzard, power outages, extreme cold, being snowed in, etc. But I didn't know what I needed to do about them . . . yet. So I researched. I jumped online and looked for answers. I asked my neighbors what I could expect. I looked at what resources, tools, and strategies were available. I also inventoried our current solutions to determine whether they were adequate for the hardships we could potentially face. The orientation phase is the research phase. But, as crucial as it is, don't get stuck here. There is more to the loop.

Decide

Once you've adequately researched and oriented yourself to the potential solutions, it's time to make a decision. This is where a lot of men get tripped up. I've seen many men get so consumed with research and analyzing their options that, although their heart is in the right place, they never end up making any decisions that will serve themselves and others best.

So, how do you know which decision to make? You choose. That's it. You take all the information at hand and you decide what you're going to do. Men who have learned to garner influence, credibility, and authority with others have learned to become decisive. Don't get trapped in paralysis by analysis. Have faith that you're capable of obtaining the information you need, evaluating it, and making good choices for you and yours. Also, know that the more decisions you make, the better you'll get at the decision-making process.

Act

Action without analysis is reckless; analysis without action is worthless. You aren't going to serve the people you care about with your intentions alone—what you "meant to do" won't help in a crisis. So execute your decision to the best of your ability. Know that it isn't going to be perfect. You're going to mess up from time to time. Never let that be a deterrent for making choices and doing everything within your power to lead others well.

As I've often said, "Leaders go first." You are a leader, or you have the potential to become one. Oftentimes, the only thing that separates the leader from the followers is a willingness to move forward in the face of adversity. Do it, and you'll set yourself apart.

It's a risk to take decisive action. If it weren't, everyone would do it. And remember, there are very few choices in life that cannot be undone or improved upon. In many cases, you can't make more effective decisions until you've proven you're willing to make the first one.

As it turns out, you don't need to predict the future at all. It's yours to create.

GET YOUR HOUSE IN ORDER

Since the dawn of men, humans have been prophesying about catastrophe. Perhaps some know more than others. Maybe our propensity to do so is a defense mechanism. Or it could just be that some are more willing to pay attention than others. Are you paying attention or are you coasting in ignorance?

If you're coasting, you're not doing yourself or those you're called to lead any service. We've all heard the phrase, "Those who are unwilling to learn from history are doomed to repeat it." It's not a matter of *if* something catastrophic will happen, but *when.*

This is why it is crucial men learn how to become an asset rather than a liability to themselves, their families, and their communities—or, as I shared earlier, to produce more than they consume. That starts with getting your house in order (in the four realms I shared in Chapter Four: physical, mental, emotional, and spiritual). As you begin to do that, you make yourself more capable of making informed, vigilant decisions on behalf of you and yours. Now, it's time to put it into practice in key domains of your life: home, office, and community.

Home

Consider all that can go wrong on the home front: sickness, disability, intruder, fire, food shortage, financial insolvency. Have you adequately prepared for the inevitable struggle at home? Have you had discussions with your family about how to deal with any of these potential situations? If you were not at home, would your family know how to handle all they could be presented with? If you cannot answer these questions in the affirmative, you have work to do:

- Secure six months' worth of food storage.
- Have cash (small bills) on hand.
- Purchase firearms and ammunition (and ensure you know how to use them properly).
- Have water available and a way to purify it.
- Make sure your medical supplies are filled.
- Ensure prescriptions and medications are addressed.
- Develop plans for an intruder.
- Develop plans for an emergency (fire, blizzard, power outage, etc.).
- Install security cameras and keep your home well lit.

Office

The office is not much different from your home. It's likely that you and your coworkers or employees spend a significant amount of time there. So why wouldn't you take care of your office space the same way you would at home? Complacency. That's the only reason. And it's no excuse.

- Install security cameras and lock doors with key fobs or security codes.
- Brief employees on responses to active shooter situations.
- Equip your team with basic medical training.

- Have food/water provisions in place.
- Develop emergency (fire, earthquake, etc.) plans.
- Put backup power plans in place.
- Ensure fire extinguishers/systems are current and charged.
- Know your team members and what emergency skill sets they possess.
- Develop evacuation plans.

Community

With as much as men are expected to shoulder, it can be easy to overlook the importance of your community, how prepared it is, and your role within it. Often, men believe they simply need to look after themselves, their families, and their friends. That said, it may pay dividends to expand your reach to your neighbors and members of your community. If they are impacted by negative circumstances that they are incapable of dealing with, the trickle-down could affect you.

- Get to know your neighbors and serve them.
- Teach what you know at your community center and/or church.
- Volunteer to put together a community watch program.
- Get to know every street, dirt road, and trail.
- If you live in a rural area, explore the woods and learn basic land navigation.
- If you live in an urban area, look for allies, escape routes, and hiding places.
- Introduce yourself to local police officers and firefighters.
- Run for school board and city council so you can enact change.

Of course, this isn't an exhaustive list of ways to get your literal and figurative house in order, but it will position you and others significantly better to handle that day you hope never happens but want to be prepared for in case it does. This is how you become an indispensable powerhouse within the walls of your home and business and in your community.

TRAPS AND TACTICS

What's most important as it relates to vigilance is that you operate as if no one is going to save you. You have to expect to self-rescue. Your ability to be prepared and think ahead will often spell the difference between success and failure.

Once again, I'm reminded of the first winter my family and I spent in Maine. The weather was getting colder, but we had not yet experienced our first snowfall. I had a business trip planned to D.C., and rather than go by myself, my wife and I thought it would make a good vacation for the kids. We decided to rent a minivan for the trip (I know, I know, I lose my man card). We had a great trip without issue until the drive home.

In the last twenty minutes before we got home, the snow started to fall. I wasn't ready for it, and the minivan lacked the tires and the four-wheel drive to handle it well. We were five miles from home, driving slowly in the thick snow up a particularly long hill. About halfway up the hill, the minivan decided it had had enough. The tires spun and spun, but regardless of how hard I pressed on the pedal, the car was stuck. I stopped, turned on the hazard lights, and tried to think of what to do. I looked at my phone. No service.

I really screwed this up! I thought. It was cold, dark, and I had put my family at risk because I wasn't as vigilant as I should have been. I noticed a plow had recently passed in the southbound lane. I was traveling north. I thought, *If I can get to that side of the road, I can make it home. But how?* As a last-ditch attempt, I floored the gas pedal, hoping the spinning tires would burn through the thin layer of snow beneath them. To my surprise, it worked. I caught just a bit of traction, pulled into the oncoming lane, and made our ascent home. We were fortunate, but it doesn't always work out that way. And sometimes the only difference is your level of vigilance in keeping yourself and others safe.

Take Inventory

What you measure will always improve. You're more likely to improve your standings in any given area if you are diligent in assessing your capabilities and skill sets and the resources at your disposal. The first step to improvement, therefore, is to track everything.

In the second section of this chapter, "Get Your House in Order," I shared twenty-six factors you can inventory and improve on. You don't have to do it all at once, but you should do it all over time. Pick one or two items each month in each of the fronts I suggested (home, office, and community), and before you know it, you'll have everything checked off the list. And you and the people you care about will be in a much better position.

Ignorance is only viable when things are going smoothly. When they're not, ignorance can be your biggest downfall. Don't be ignorant. Know where you stand and where you need to improve.

Interview Others

I've made a career out of interviewing successful men, and as much as I hope the conversations we have serve those who listen, I've always felt as if I'm the greatest beneficiary of the work we're doing.

Every week, I get to talk one-on-one with some of the most successful people on the planet, from *New York Times* bestselling authors to top athletes to highly successful entrepreneurs and everything in between.

There is a wealth of knowledge everywhere, and all you have to do is tap into it. Don't ever let a great opportunity to learn from someone else go to waste. Find qualified people in your network and ask them about their life, their expertise, and what tips they'd give you to be successful in any given field. Approach others with a genuine level of curiosity and the objective to grow your own capabilities. Men have always been social animals. For good reason—we're stronger together. Utilize your network effectively.

Survey Your Surroundings

Whenever I'm out with my children, we play a game. I challenge them to survey the area we're in and ask them questions about a scenario they may expect to encounter. "If someone came in here waving a gun around, what would you do?" "If you got separated from us, who would you approach and why?" "What can you tell about that particular person just by looking at them?" "Where is the safest place in this store?" I've asked them thousands of questions over the course of their lives. Some they get correct. Others, they do not. But the game always starts with the premise of observing their surroundings. Over time, they've improved their abilities to accurately assess their environment.

We, as men, need to be doing the same for ourselves. I cannot believe how many men I've observed who are completely oblivious to their surroundings. I've watched people run into poles and parked cars. I've seen them inadvertently ignore someone who may have asked a question. I've seen them trip over their own untied shoelaces. It's incredible how much people miss because their heads are buried in their phones or they don't take a little time to orient themselves to their environment. Don't be that guy.

Whenever you're somewhere new, do a quick scan to look for things that might be off: bad actors who would make you their target, and dangers that might otherwise be overlooked. It doesn't take more than a few seconds, and doing so is the mark of a vigilant man.

Expect the Best, Prepare for the Worst

The odds are, you're not going to find yourself in any serious danger. You're not likely going to encounter a violent person. No one is likely to break into your home. For the most part, you're going to keep yourself out of nature's destructive path. That, however, is no reason not to be prepared for these types of situations, because when they do happen, they happen fast, and they can be catastrophic.

Anticipate the things that could go wrong and make a plan to deal with them. Have you secured your home and office with locks, security cameras, and lighting? Have you stocked your shelves with food storage in the event you're stuck inside or there is a food shortage? Have you walked through home evacuation with your children? Do you have the right tools and equipment in your vehicle should you break down on the side of the road?

Get your mindset right because when things go south, people are going to look to you. You don't need to become a pessimist or obsessed with it, but you should never find yourself in a situation you haven't actively thought about and made plans for dealing with.

CHAPTER THIRTEEN

VIOLENCE

It is better to be a warrior in a garden than a gardener in war.

—*Chinese Proverb*

No man ever took pride in being weak and incapable of physically defending himself and those he cares about. He may have conveniently convinced himself that a true man is "civil" and has no need for violence in modern culture. But I would contend that the proliferation of civility as the noblest of virtues is what got us into a lot of the mess that we're currently in.

With the government overextending its reach by infusing trillions of dollars into the already-inflated economy; organizations like Black Lives Matter, whose radical agenda promotes rioting and looting to the tune of billions of dollars' worth of property destroyed; the "Defund the Police" nonsense that has led to a rise in crime across major U.S. cities; and school boards across the country advocating for woke policy, dangerous gender ideology, and Critical Race Theory, it's clear to me that the powers that be believe there is little accountability and/or resistance to their insidious objectives. They also believe that we'll quietly and politely let the rights our forefathers fought and died for slip through our fingers.

And they may be right.

Civility serves a purpose. It truly does. It has paved the way for the most prosperous time in human history, ushering in advancements in life-saving medical equipment, procedures, and medicine as well as advancements in technology that allow us to be more connected than ever. Civility has granted us access to an abundance of wealth that has lifted more humans out of abject poverty than ever before.

So where does this leave us in striking the balance between our masculine urge to solve problems with violence and utilizing civility to advance ourselves and the people we care about? The answer is simple: we need both—the ability to administer righteous violence should the situation call for it *and* the prowess to exercise a civil response to the conflict between our desires and others'.

As Jordan Peterson famously said, "A harmless man is not a good man. A good man is a very dangerous man who has that under voluntary control."[1] He also said, "You should be a monster, an absolute monster, and then you should learn how to control it."[2]

In many ways, the modern man has been led to believe, and fooled himself into thinking, that being affable is the highest virtue he could strive for. It isn't. Likeability is often a clever cloak for weakness. That is not exclusively true, however. Some of the most dangerous men I know are also the kindest. But if a man has no alternative to civility for obtaining his desires, he lacks a masculine depth that will allow him to protect and serve himself and others in any and every situation.

Besides, there is a chance you will, at some point in your life, be confronted with violence. If you aren't intimately already familiar with it, there is a strong likelihood you'll cower when you should stand. The popular narrative is that the violent perpetrator needs love, help, or direction. This is part of the reason we see such an emphasis on "Defund the Police" movements and calls for social workers to respond to these dangerous encounters rather than cops. What those advocates fail to realize is the nature of violence and how much hate and anger are in some people's souls. Refusing to acknowledge and adequately prepare yourself for violence will not protect you from it.

Edmund Burke once said, "The only thing necessary for the triumph of evil is for good men to do nothing." I would also add, "and being *incapable* of doing something." Interestingly enough, simply knowing how to be violent in the right circumstances may keep a situation from escalating altogether.

Case in point: Last year my oldest son and I pulled into a gas station to fill up my truck. I got out of the truck, put my credit card into the pump, and began pumping gas. It was a cold winter day, so as the pump was going, I got back into the cab of my truck.

Not a minute went by before I heard someone yelling behind me. My son said, "Dad, that guy is yelling at you." I turned to see what the commotion was all about it. Two men on snowmobiles were cursing and pointing at me. I had no idea why. As I turned around, they whipped their snowmobiles to the side of my truck. "Why the f*** didn't you pull up, a**hole?" one guy shouted. "Can't you see we're waiting here?"

Apparently, the guy thought I should have pulled up to the first pump so he could pull behind me. I would have, but the first pump was out of order—something the snowmobilers could not see from where they were. I explained that to him and pointed to the pump. He jerked his snowmobile in front of my truck, took off his helmet, and approached the passenger side of the truck where my son was.

This isn't happening, I thought. I opened my truck door and kept an eye on the second man as I did. He was sheepishly fiddling with his machine. (I think he knew how dumb they looked.) I turned to the first guy. "Get away from my truck and get back on your snowmobile." I wasn't overly emotional. I didn't scream at him. In fact, I remember being very calm, but I made sure he knew I meant what I said. Head down, mumbling under his breath, he walked away from my truck and slunk into the convenience store. My son and I finished pumping gas and drove off without further issue.

I don't know why he stepped down. Maybe he thought it was as stupid as I did. Or perhaps he heard something in my voice and saw something in my demeanor that let him know I was willing and capable of defending myself and my son. Regardless, my ability to stand up for myself and my son kept us out of harm's way that day. In a similar situation, a man who cannot defend himself might have had a completely different result.

I don't want to fight. I don't want to be violent. That isn't my default. I'd choose to stay out of physical altercations if I could (and I have for the most part). But you can be sure I'm not willing to be a victim if someone puts me and my family and friends in harm's way. No man should be.

WARRIOR IN THE GARDEN

We've all heard the Chinese proverb, "It is better to be a warrior in a garden than a gardener in war." I believe that's true. How could it not be? Which man is at greater risk if he is not skilled in the other's profession: the warrior who doesn't know how to garden or the gardener who doesn't know how to fight?

Another of my favorite quotes as it pertains to violence comes from Roman author Publius Flavius Vegetius Renatus. In Latin, it is *Igitur qui desiderat pacem, praeparet bellum*, which is translated as, "If you want peace, prepare for war."

The reality is that we, as men, are made for combat. We're bigger, stronger, and faster than our female counterparts. We've always been the protectors—the guardians of ourselves, our families, and our people. That hasn't changed simply because our likelihood of dealing with a violent encounter has drastically decreased in modern history. Statistically, you're much less likely to have to defend yourself against another person than you were even a hundred or two hundred years ago. But the statistics don't matter much if you find yourself facing a violent encounter.

A man's job is to recognize, manage, and mitigate risk to himself and others. That is a key element of the service a man provides to his family, coworkers, and neighbors.

Unfortunately, we've all heard stories of men who find themselves wholly unqualified to deal with someone who wishes to harm them and those they're tasked to serve. Do not let that be you. Be the protector you're capable of becoming, and you will garner the respect you deserve from those who look to you when things go south.

In order to do that, you're going to have to level the playing field against others who would love nothing more than to make you their victim. If you've ever found yourself in a dangerous encounter with another, you know they don't care about the so-called "rules" you play by. All they want to do is hurt, maim, destroy, and kill. Violence does not care about fair. Violence does not care about your goals, ambitions, desires, and potential. Violence does not care that you are unprepared. In fact, it banks on it. And ignorance is not going to get you and others out of harm's way.

But there is one thing that might: your ability to meet your attacker where they are and fight fire with fire. Again, violence isn't something men hope for, but it is something they're capable of dealing with and administering in their own way. Men are familiar with and proficient in the resources of a fighter: mind, body, and tools.

Mind

If you can develop the mindset of a warrior, you're much more likely to keep yourself and others out of danger. Your mind and wits are the first level of defense against the violence you may meet. And, many times, you can deescalate or avoid a dangerous situation altogether just by exercising a little critical thinking and knowing the mind of a would-be attacker.

This is part of the reason it's so crucial you become familiar with violence. It's easy to spot and avoid if you know what to look out for (see Chapter Twelve, "Vigilance").

Body

Your body can and should be trained to keep you and others safe. First, are you physically fit? If not, you're a much easier target to deal with. There is no other way to say it. If you've got a few extra pounds or more around the midsection, you cannot possibly be as effective as someone else who is lean and strong.

Second, do you know how to fight? Can you throw a punch? Can you take someone down to the ground and subdue or disengage? And no, you aren't miraculously going to become Jason Bourne in the moment. You have to train to make your body a weapon. What does your training (or lack thereof) say about you and your ability to successfully navigate a dangerous and violent situation?

Tools

There are many tools you can use to keep yourself and others safe, but there is nothing quite as effective at leveling the playing field as a firearm. Every man ought to be familiar with how they work, what they're capable of, and how to operate one. I often meet both men and women who aren't comfortable with the prospect of handling a firearm. Fine. Again, the way you feel about it doesn't matter. Not learning to use a firearm because you're uncomfortable with one would be like saying you're not going to learn to swim because you don't like the water.

Besides, the more you operate any tool, the more familiar and comfortable you become with it. It's no different with a knife, a crowbar, or any number of day-to-day objects that could become a useful weapon in the right situation. Carpenters know how to swing a hammer. Coders know how to use a computer. Photographers know how to use a camera. Men know how to use weapons. Scottish historian Thomas Carlyle once said, "Man is a tool-using animal; without tools he is nothing, with tools he is all."

At the end of the day, you never know what kind of situation you or your people are going to meet, so it's just best to "be a warrior in the garden." And if you never find yourself having to administer righteous violence to someone who wishes to administer evil violence to you, good—but there are many other benefits to knowing how.

THE SOFTER SIDE OF VIOLENCE

There is another, often overlooked side of violence that every man needs to tap into. I've only recently found this for myself when I started training in Jiu-Jitsu regularly.

I began training at the recommendation of three of my friends: Matthew Arrington, Kipp Sorensen, and Pete Roberts. Initially, I wanted to learn Jiu-Jitsu because I believed it would help me defend myself in a violent encounter with another man. And while the value of that is certainly significant, I quickly learned that there are so many other softer, much harder to quantify benefits of training not just Jiu-Jitsu but martial arts in general.

I've learned more about who I truly am and how to make myself more of a man through controlled violence than just about any other practice I've been involved in. You find out pretty quickly what you're made of when another strong, capable man attempts to attack one of your limbs or wraps his arms around your neck to squeeze the life out of you.

By nature, men are designed to be physical. And I believe that a man can never fully remove the propensity for violence from his blood. I don't believe he should even try. It seems to me that if a man continually suppresses that part of his nature, it's a recipe for disaster. Down the road, that nature will reveal itself in unbridled and inappropriate ways—like punching a wall, or worse, someone you care about in a moment of frustration or anger. Men are much better served by learning to harness their violence than trying to suppress it.

I learned this lesson when I was in high school. I always played sports and was fairly athletic. I particularly enjoyed football and baseball. I tried out for the basketball team my sophomore year. Not because I liked basketball, but because that's where all my friends were. Unfortunately, I got cut. It was rough for me because I lost the physical outlet I needed to relieve the frustrations and aggression of my day-to-day life. I started getting in fights to deal with it. Needless to say, that led to a host of other problems that derailed me from who I wanted to be.

Sensing I needed a more productive outlet, one of my coaches approached me and said, "Ryan, you need to try out for the wrestling team, or you won't play football for me next year." I'm so glad he did. I found the outlet I needed, and my life and attitude began to improve almost overnight.

Again, that outlet was stripped away from me after high school, and I learned to deal with my aggressive (and often violent) nature by hiding it. Nineteen years later, I found Jiu-Jitsu, and for the first time in nearly two decades, I was asked not to hide my nature but to exercise it in a controlled environment. My only regret is that I wish I hadn't wasted two decades pretending to be a "nice guy" while my rage boiled just under the surface, ready to erupt at the slightest grievance.

Becoming familiar with and embracing violence (there isn't a better way to say it) through Jiu-Jitsu has made me a much more well-rounded, even-keeled man. It's infinitely harder to get me upset when I spend one to two hours four to five times per week with other men who expect me to do everything I can to best them as they attempt to do the same to me.

I've learned patience, critical thinking, how to slow down my breathing, how to think in stressful situations, discipline, commitment, dedication, humility, how not to get hurt, how to keep myself safe and protected, and a laundry list of other benefits too long to mention.

Who would have imagined that embracing violence would lead to such productive outcomes? Well, just about every civilization before this modern one, apparently. Take a young boy's desire to roughhouse with his father or other boys his age. It's abundantly clear that young girls don't have the desire to fight the same way boys do. And yet, what does society do when it sees two boys fighting, even in play? It sedates them with harmful medication and asks them to behave more like their female counterparts.

I often think of the proliferation of school shootings, most of which are carried out by boys without a strong manly presence in their lives, and wonder if things would have been different had they had the luxury of a father in their lives to fight and wrestle with.

Some of the angriest people I know are often the weakest and most incapable, and conversely, some of the deadliest men I know are the kindest and calmest. That is the softer side of violence. Embracing it is a tempering mechanism for the nature of men. Our propensity to be physical never goes away. It simply lies dormant while we uselessly attempt to keep it from rearing its ugly head. Instead, we ought to become more familiar with our violent nature so we can control it and keep it from controlling us.

You don't want to be angry? Simple. Fight more.

TRAPS AND TACTICS

As I said earlier, men don't go out seeking violence, but they ought to be prepared for it if it comes seeking them. There is no excuse, if you wish to call yourself a man, for not knowing how to handle it when it comes knocking on your door. It's not as if you can call a timeout to regroup and consider your best defense in the moment. No, that day is like a pop quiz, and you're going to find out the hard way if you are prepared or not. Make sure you find yourself and others on the winning side of that equation.

Know What You're Walking Into

Get familiar with violence. Study it. Read books on it. As great sports teams watch film to prepare for their next contest, you too should watch, analyze, and critique violent encounters. Ignorance isn't going to serve you and others, but becoming intimately familiar with the mind, tools, and tactics of a would-be attacker just might. Retired U.S. Army Lieutenant Colonel Dave Grossman has written two books every man ought to read on the psychology of violence: *On Combat* and *On Killing*. Read them both and familiarize yourself with the situations you hope you never find yourself in but don't want to be found wanting if you do.

Train Martial Arts

Your body is a weapon, or at least it could be. Find a place in your area to train martial arts. I'm not going to get into which practice is best and why, because they all serve their purpose, whether it's boxing, kick-boxing, Muay Thai, Jiu-Jitsu, wrestling, Krav Maga, or any number of other combat sports you can participate in. As I mentioned earlier, I personally train Jiu-Jitsu, but I see the value of most combat sports. The key is to find a reputable school and get involved in the discipline you'll stay committed to. As with anything, it takes time to build a skill set. You aren't going to move the needle by simply showing up to a class or two. Commit to making it a way of life, even if you can only train one or two days per week.

Buy a Firearm and Train with It

I would suggest that if you aren't familiar with firearms, go to your local gun shop and ask which firearm is right for self-defense. With so many to choose from, it's hard to know which route to go, especially if you haven't shot much or at all. You may also want to look for a reputable gun range that will let you shoot a wide selection of firearms so you can get a feel for which one is right for you before you buy. At many of these ranges, you can hire a firearms instructor to help you navigate the waters if you're new to shooting. Don't just buy a firearm and place it on a shelf. Become proficient with it. Train with it frequently and know how to store it safely and appropriately to keep it away from those who shouldn't have access to it but ready should you need it.

Teach Your People

Great leaders have the heart of a teacher. And if you believe for one second that you're going to be the hero of the day in some violent encounter, you may want to think again. What if you're not around? What if you go down and become incapacitated? What if you're dead? Any leader worth his weight knows that he has a responsibility to empower his family members, neighbors, colleagues, and employees.

Have your family train martial arts with you. Buy some inexpensive mats off Amazon to have in your home so you can wrestle, box, and fight with your kids. Consider subsidizing the cost of martial arts or firearms training for your employees. Do whatever you can to serve others by ensuring that they can serve themselves. Who knows? Someone you've helped might end up saving you.

CHAPTER FOURTEEN

HONESTY

Honesty is the first chapter in the book of wisdom.

—*Thomas Jefferson*

There are very few traits as important as honesty when it comes to garnering the influence, authority, and credibility required to lead well. And there is nothing that undermines it as quickly as developing a reputation as a liar. But equally as crushing as being viewed as a man with integrity issues is being labeled a coward.

Once you strip everything away, what lies at the root of deceit is cowardice. The only reason a man is unwilling to tell the truth is fear of the consequences for doing so. He is afraid of judgment. He is afraid of losing something he loves. He is afraid of hurting other people. (That's what he thinks, anyway. More on that later.) Ironically, a man who tells the truth in spite of the consequences he may suffer ends up not being judged less favorably but building trust, not losing what he holds dear but securing more in his life, and not hurting others but serving them more effectively.

If cowardice lies at the foundation of deception, the only way to overcome it is by exercising courage. Courage is the antidote to cowardice, and courage is all that is required to tell the truth. It takes courage because there is an overwhelming amount of risk involved with being honest.

If, for example, you are willing to tell yourself the truth about your current underperformance, you risk having to either a) do something about it or b) live with knowing you're not as good as you could otherwise be. If you feel compelled to speak truthfully about someone under your care, you risk their being upset with you for drawing attention to something they wish to keep hidden. If you feel inclined to speak the truth against many of the woke narratives you hear in popular culture today, you risk backlash, public doxxing, and even financial consequences for doing so.

But the truth is more important than the consequences you may face for being an honest man. Unfortunately, the world is filled with liars and cowards. And we have the audacity to wonder why we're facing such a crisis in masculine leadership? It's pretty simple. Can you name *one* coward you wish to follow? Of course not.

As the saying goes, "Fortune favors the brave." Also, influence favors the honest. There's a reason for that. Influence is afforded to those who are honest, because a man's honesty is directly proportionate to his level of care for others.

That may seem a bit counterintuitive, but stay with me on this. It's easy to deceive yourself. We tell ourselves all sorts of lies, stories, and excuses, and rationalize the things we do. But when we lie, we're not really worried about others, are we? It's a self-preservation tactic. If you step out on your wife, you're not likely to be anxious to come clean because you're concerned that she may leave you if you do. And if that's the concern, can you really say that you're worried about her well-being? Or is yours what you're really concerned about?

Let me give you another example. Early in my financial planning career, I was desperate to build my business. So much so that, at times, I would begin working with a client after I knew that the solutions my business offered were not solutions that person needed. The best thing I could have done at the time was to admit that we did *not* have a solution for their problems and direct them to someone who did. By attempting to make them my clients, I wasn't doing them any favors. In fact, I was doing them a disservice. But as much as I hate to admit it, it was only because I cared more about my own interests than I did theirs. That's no way to build a solid reputation with others.

Trust and honesty require you to put the needs of others above your own. If you can't do that, don't you dare call yourself a leader of others.

Truth also requires you to look at life and your service to others through a long lens. Honesty demands you see the broader picture before you make your day-to-day decisions. Truth requires you to dream big but play small. What I mean is that in order to be truthful with yourself and others, you have to maintain a long-term perspective of how the truth will serve you and others into the future. If all you care about is what happens *now*, you'll be more likely to lie, stretch the truth, or lie by omission. You may even convince yourself you're doing the right thing by smoothing over a temporary situation, but at what cost? I'll tell you: your influence, credibility, and authority with others.

HONOR YOURSELF AND YOUR PEOPLE

So, let's talk about the word *honesty*, which obviously derives from the same root as *honorable*. The word *honesty* can be traced back thousands of years to the Latin *honestus* and the Old French *oneste*, and can be defined as "respect," "dignity," "distinction," "reputation," and "free from fraud." The word *honor* can be defined as "glory," "renown," "fame earned," and "show respect to."

So how do men honor or "show respect to" themselves, their families, their friends, and their community members? By being honest or "free from fraud." In other words, a man honors himself and others by caring enough about them not to deceive them. Truth is the ultimate sign of service to others.

Service is an interesting concept. The word has been hijacked to mean "to do something noble or significant." While I agree there is value in being noble, that alone is not enough. To serve, you must sacrifice. It is not service if no sacrifice is required and offered.

Truth requires sacrifice. It requires you to sacrifice other people's feelings. It requires you to sacrifice the way you feel yourself. It requires you to say and do what needs to be said and done so that others may live more fully.

Two years ago, my oldest son approached me and my wife. For several months leading up to that conversation, he had been feeling pretty down on himself for the way he looked. I could certainly understand his frustration. He had really let his eating and lack of exercise get out of hand.

"Mom and Dad," he said, "I don't feel good about myself. I feel fat."

A moment of truth. And what my wife and I said and did next would have real implications in the way he viewed himself and the way he lived his life.

It would have been easy for us to say, "No, son, you're not fat. You're special and important just the way you are. You need to learn to love yourself how you are."

But that wasn't true. It may have come from a place of good intentions and our deep care for and devotion to him, but it was not true. The truth was that he had packed on a few pounds and really did need to do something about it. So, rather than lie to him, we decided to tell him the truth and help him develop eating and exercise habits that would actually help him, not just put a Band-Aid on the way he viewed his current self.

Over the past several years, he has completely transformed himself from a timid little roly-poly to a confident, fit young man, which all started from a place of truth, not delusion.

Truth, after all, is the bedrock of growth. You cannot grow (or expect others to) if you are unwilling to face the reality of the current situation. But if you truly want to honor yourself and others, that's exactly what you'll do—confront reality.

This shows up in so many ways in our lives as we work to serve and lead others well:

- When your coworker drops the ball on the assignment, do you sweep it under the rug?
- When your client doesn't uphold their end of the deal, do you say something?
- When you slack off on your own work, do you acknowledge or justify it?
- When you say you'll help your friend move, do you show up?
- When you've cheated others, do you admit it and make it right?
- When your child asks about sex or porn, do you address it or deflect it?

We all know what the answer to the above questions should be, and yet we often struggle to align our actions with what we know to be right. Why do we do that? It isn't that you don't care about the people in your life. You do. It's that you care more about yourself than you do them. You might jump to disagree with me on that. "Ryan, you're telling me I care more about myself than I do my own children?" If you aren't willing to tell them the truth, yes, that's exactly what I'm saying.

Let's say one of your children asks about a topic you're not really interested in discussing. Don't you believe that your children will be served if you answer their inquiries? Of course they will. But many men aren't willing to do it—not because they want their kids to remain ignorant, but because they themselves can't handle the discomfort of the conversation. Their unwillingness to have an awkward conversation has nothing to do with their children and everything to do with them. That isn't service. That's selfishness.

The only reason you wouldn't tell the truth to a coworker isn't because you don't want them to feel bad. It's because you don't want to *make* them feel bad. Again, selfishness.

If you've cheated someone else, the only reason you're not willing to make amends is because you know you'll have to sacrifice your own dignity to do so. News flash, you already have by engaging in the action in the first place. Now, the only way to restore it is to make the situation right. You already know how doing the right thing will make other people feel. That's not the question. The question is whether you're honorable enough to sacrifice yourself for the betterment of others.

You honor people by telling them the truth. Yes, there are many instances where it's going to be painful to do so, but as I discussed earlier, service requires sacrifice. And service to others will establish influence, authority, and credibility more effectively than anything else.

But there is another major reason to be honest, especially in a world filled with dishonesty.

BECOME A BEACON OF TRUTH

I receive hundreds of messages a week from the men and women who listen to the *Order of Man* podcast. While I'm grateful for 99.7 percent of the messages I receive (the remaining 0.3 percent represents the trolls who hate themselves and everyone else), there is one particular type of message I really appreciate. It goes something like this:

"Ryan, I wanted to let you know that I don't agree with everything you say. But even in disagreement, I respect that you are so firm in your convictions. Keep doing the work you're doing."

It certainly strokes the ego to know that what you're putting out into the world is resonating with people, but the reason I really appreciate this type of message is because it lets me know there is a level of respect afforded to me even though the sender and I would disagree on a few key issues.

I'm really trying to put good work and information out into the world, and although there is plenty to contend with regarding what my guests and I share, I do make a sincere effort to be honest.

If I don't know something, I'm willing to say, "I don't know." If I believe a certain way about a particularly charged issue, I'm willing to share it respectfully with those who would listen. I know the difference between "the Truth" (with a capital *T*) and "my opinion," and I'm always straightforward with that.

But this message isn't about me. It's about you. I want you to garner the respect and influence you desire and deserve. In order to do that, you have to learn to tell the truth. It's a bit counterintuitive that the truth will always prevail. It's tempting to believe that you can deceive your way into influence, authority, and credibility. And maybe you can . . . temporarily. But if you're building it all on lies and deception, you're building your level of respect on a faulty footing. Believe me, you will be found out.

You can build an incredible amount of respect by being a man who speaks the truth. Even though you'll find many people who disagree with you, you will be amazed at how often the dissenters will respect you for being a man of conviction.

The reality is that you're not going to win everyone over. Some people aren't interested in being "won over." Others find a twisted sense of satisfaction in proving you wrong and contending with you on every single issue. But in a world filled with spineless cowards who change their narrative based on who they're talking to, you can become a man who is steadfast and resolute in truth and the discovery of it.

I've built an incredible business and movement on nothing more than curiosity regarding what it means to be a man, and you would be surprised to learn how many people follow the podcast, join our programs, attend our events, buy our books, and stay connected with us who originally thought I was full of crap.

Influence, authority, and credibility are not fickle factors. They take a long time to establish, and once you possess them, it takes quite a bit to erode the base you have built.

Telling the truth isn't always popular. Some of the most hated men throughout history have been the men who were willing to tell the truth in spite of how people felt about it. Feelings, unfortunately, are what drive most of the decisions we individually and collectively make these days. If you're a man who's willing to be a truth-teller, you have to know that the masses will not like you.

But do you know who will like you? The men and women like you. The ones who value a man with a spine. The people who want to grow a spine themselves. Those are the people who matter.

You're going to run across a lot of immature, irrational crybabies on your path to becoming the man you're meant to be. You're going to be tempted to try to win them over with cheap tricks. Don't. Stand firm. Stand resolute. The people who matter will find you, and you'll win over a few who have been waiting for someone—anyone—to stand as a beacon of truth.

TRAPS AND TACTICS

Honesty is such a rare quality today that it will quickly set you apart as a man to be trusted. I realize that telling the truth isn't always easy to do. I suppose that if it were, you'd see more honesty in the world.

But most people are driven by their own selfish desires, and while there is nothing wrong with having personal goals and ambitions, if success requires you to lie to others, there is going to be hell to pay. Maybe not now, but certainly in the future. The truth of the situation is that you can only fool people for so long. But why would you want to do that, anyway? That's no way to establish the credibility you're after. You'll find yourself alone and miserable if you build your relationships on a foundation of deceit.

It's much better for you and those you are working to serve to build your relationships on a foundation of truth and honesty. It will take longer to yield the fruit you're after, but if you plant your tree in the right soil (honesty), you'll be harvesting long after the weaklings', cowards', and liars' crops have dried up and died.

All that said, there is a right way to do it and a wrong way to do it. Choose wisely.

Know the Difference between "The Truth" and "Your Opinion"

You've likely heard the popular catchphrase "my truth." It sounds clever, but it's not real. There is no "my truth." There is only the truth and your perception (or opinion) of it. It's crucial you know the difference because it's possible to deceive others in ignorance or with good intentions. Those you have influence over will often perceive your opinion to be truth if you're not willing to acknowledge the difference.

Besides, I'm not really sure when having an opinion about something went out of style, but I can assure you, it is perfectly acceptable to have an opinion about something or perceive a set of circumstances through your own personal lens of culture, background, experience, religion, etc. In fact, your opinion and perception of reality are paramount in the grand scheme of things. Coupled with thousands or millions of other opinions, we get close to the truth or, at least, solutions that will collectively serve us more effectively.

In January 2022, I sat down and recorded a conversation with legendary radio, TV, and podcast host Adam Carolla. We discussed this very issue, and while Adam did not discount the importance of people's opinions, he did suggest that opinions should change over time in light of new information and/or a level of maturity that comes with age and experience.

Don't undermine yourself with others by misinterpreting your opinion as unequivocal truth. It isn't. Recognize the truth for what it is. Recognize your perception of it for what it is. You can't be a man of honesty if you can't distinguish fact from fiction.

Be Cautious in Offering Unsolicited Feedback

Is there an instance in all of human history where an individual appreciated unsolicited feedback? I would think not. Think about the last time someone shared some insight with you that you didn't ask for. How did that pan out? That's not to say you shouldn't be receptive to poorly delivered information that will serve you. I'm suggesting you personally avoid the trap of offering feedback that wasn't asked for and certainly will not be appreciated.

But let's also be clear that if someone works directly for you or is under your direct care (your children, for example), not only should you offer feedback, but you have a responsibility and obligation to do so. These individuals do not need to give you their express permission to offer some constructive criticism or feedback. It's inherent in the type of relationship you have that you will.

But for those who are not under your direct care, tread lightly when you feel the need to offer advice that was not asked for. And consider evaluating why you feel the need to do so in the first place. Is it ego driven? Do you like to hear the sound of your own voice? Do you think you know better than another whom you may not fully understand or whose situation you may not fully appreciate?

Or do you genuinely want to help someone with a problem they are dealing with? If that's the case, I would highly encourage you to secure permission to offer feedback before you stick your foot in your mouth. Then, and only then, should you consider gracing others with your opinion. Even then, there's a way to do it correctly.

Tell the Truth, but Don't Be a Dick

It seems to me there is a growing sentiment (especially in the men's self-help space) that in order to be truthful with others, you're required to be a jerk about it. If you don't believe what I'm saying, consider the mentality of men who profess not to care at all about what other people think of them, or the last time you heard a man shout, "That's just how I am. If people don't like it, that's their problem!" It sounds tough, but it's stupid.

For anyone who's proclaimed either, are you willing to tell me that you're so immature and incapable of adapting your delivery to different people that you're completely content with shooting yourself in the foot every time you offer feedback to others? That's the real issue. That brazen attitude with others isn't going to move the needle. That's what you're after, right? To get the project moving. To get your children to clean their room. To develop influence with your wife. To secure the job or promotion. To pick up that new client.

You've got to meet people where they are and communicate with them in a way that gets the ball rolling in the right direction. That's not to say you need to change *who* you are in order to do so, but you may want to, at a minimum, consider *how* you do it. A mature man understands this and uses language, nonverbal communication, and tact tools to produce the desired result. An immature man simply cries about why no one respects him.

If People Ask for Your Opinion, Give It

This sounds simple enough, but it proves to be a constant challenge for many men. Stating your opinion comes with the risk that someone will see things differently, leading to a potential confrontation. As I mentioned in Chapter Eleven, "Aggression," most people are afraid of confrontation, so they have a difficult time expressing themselves.

Men need to learn to express themselves more effectively in spite of the associated risk. The best way to do that is to force yourself to share your opinion when asked. Do not deflect. Do not say you don't care or pretend as if you're indifferent to the situation (that's lying). The truth is that you *do* care and you *do* have an opinion in any given moment. So share it.

A very easy way to practice this is in a nonthreatening environment. Next time one of your coworkers asks where you would like to go for lunch, tell them *exactly* where you want to go. Next time your wife asks what show you'd like to watch or what you'd like to do tonight, tell her *exactly* what you'd like to do. Next time a colleague asks what you would do with a project they've been tasked with, tell them *exactly* what you would do. Again, no deflecting, no indifference, no cowering. Be bold. Be assertive. Tell the truth, which is that you *do* have an opinion, a perspective, and an interest in taking charge of your life.

CHAPTER FIFTEEN

SELF-RESPECT

I count him braver who overcomes his desires than him who conquers his enemies; for the hardest victory is over self.

—*Aristotle*

saved self-respect for the last of the eight characteristics of masculinity because it might just be the most important topic we discuss in this book. If a man can learn to develop a healthy level of self-respect, everything else we've talked about here will begin to fall into place.

A man who respects himself will more effectively use the mindsets of masculine leadership and his masculinity in general. He will be more assertive, more confident, and bolder in his approach to his own life and to leading others.

Besides, no one is ever going to have more respect for you than you have for yourself. They may feel sorry for you. They may have pity on you. They may even want to serve and help you. But make no mistake, that has less to do with how they see you as a leader and more to do with their desire to be good and decent human beings.

Men aren't interested in handouts anyway, and they sure don't take pride in being treated like a wounded animal some passerby saw abandoned on the side of the road.

Also, the more you sense that others feel sorry for you, the more likely you are to undermine your own self-respect and dignity. It's a vicious cycle. You feel bad about your performance and yourself, others begin to feel bad for you, and you feel bad because others feel bad for you. And the cycle continues until you find a way to break free from the cage of depression you built for yourself.

But there is a common misconception about self-respect. Some men seem to believe that it's reserved exclusively for a lucky few. They may look around at other men whom they perceive to have some sort of mystical X factor and wonder why they can't seem to ever possess it for themselves. It's become so elusive that many men have resigned to live in constant doubt about who they are as men and how they show up.

It doesn't have to be a mystery, and self-respect isn't reserved for the lucky. That said, it cannot be borrowed. It cannot be given by someone else. It must be earned. It's a lonely venture, and not a single person can help you develop self-respect beyond teaching you how to discover it for yourself. It's all on your shoulders, where it belongs. That's the bad news. The good news is that you have the ability to control only yourself, and that's all you need.

I speak from experience. Twelve years ago, I was fat, miserable, broke, and lonely. I was in a state of despair as my health had deteriorated, my financial planning practice was struggling, and my wife had left with my one-year-old son. I felt unappreciated, unloved, and unwanted. I thought if only someone would help me, I would feel better about myself. It didn't work. I had friends and relatives who would try to cheer me up and support me, but nothing seemed to reach me in the pit of despair I found myself in.

It didn't change for me until I realized that if I was the source of all my problems, then I had the power to be the source of my solutions. I didn't need anyone else to help me find my dignity. I needed to create it from the ground up. I began to look at it like lifting weights. You cannot have someone else do deadlifts for you and expect to get stronger. It's all on you. And what you do or don't do will determine your success or lack thereof.

What was interesting was that as I began to build my self-respect, people began to respond positively to me.

I saw this play out in real time in my financial planning practice. I was so desperate early on in my career to get new clients, I would do and say anything I could and even almost beg for business. It was pathetic. My potential clients were repelled by it, and I couldn't seem to figure out why I couldn't grow my practice the way others around me were growing theirs.

As I went to work on myself, I began to develop a healthy sense of identity. As if I'd flipped a switch, my external surroundings changed almost immediately. My clients began to see me in a new light. Now, instead of being repulsed by my low level of self-worth, they were drawn like a magnet to the self-respect (and corresponding confidence) I had developed. It has continued to play out in every facet of my life from clients to winning back the affection of my wife to leading my children and even to starting a podcast, securing guests, and growing our audience to millions of men around the world.

It may seem miraculous, but it really isn't. There is nothing mystical to it. It's a simple formula that, once learned, can be repeated in every facet of your life.

WIN THE BATTLE WITH YOURSELF

In Chapter Two, I introduced you to the concept of the *natural man*. As I said, he is the weaker, lesser, more pathetic version of yourself. You know exactly who he is. He is within every man. He's not *you*, per se, but he is *part* of you or, at a minimum, who you have a natural inclination to become. But also within you is the ability to do and become more. This is the man who is driven and hard-charging. This is the man who knows what he wants and is willing to do what it takes to achieve it. This is the man who doesn't look at other people as pawns on his journey to self-actualization, but as partners he can serve along his personal path.

The second man is who you have the potential to become. The first is who you might be more closely aligned with today.

The first man—the natural man—is self-absorbed. He cares only about his own progress but, ironically, is unwilling to do anything about it. He believes his results should be bestowed upon him. He believes being male is enough. He's entitled, spoiled, and self-righteous.

The second man—the man you have the potential to become—is the antithesis of the natural man. He cares about his progress but not at the expense of others. He believes his results are a manifestation of the work he does (or doesn't do). He believes that being a man is something worth striving toward. He's selfless, generous, and humble.

Both are unrealized versions of yourself. You are not destined to become either. What you do today, tomorrow, and every day moving forward will determine which of the two men you become.

So who wins the battle between these two versions? I can't answer that question. Only you can. And time will tell which version you align with. What I can tell you is that a battle between the two takes place every day.

When the alarm goes off in the morning, the natural man will hit snooze. The better man will not. When confronted with a challenge, the natural man will run away and hide or sedate himself with drugs, alcohol, pornography, and other distractions. The better man will face his fear head-on and confront the challenge. When presented with an idea that could change his life and the lives of others, the natural man will slink away into obscurity. The better man will rise to embrace the opportunity and all the hardship that comes with it.

In short, the natural man hates himself because he knows he is not the man he could be. The better man loves himself because he knows he is on the path to realizing his best self.

The natural man will never respect himself. He isn't a man worth respecting. He knows this. The better man is filled with self-respect because he's done the work required to garner it from both himself and others.

Each moment of each day is an opportunity to prove to yourself who you really are. Make good choices from the minute you wake up to the minute your head hits the pillow. Inevitably, people will ask me what is "good" and what is "right." I hesitate to answer those questions because you already know what you need to do. You may not know the specific details, but you know which direction you should be heading in.

The only choice that remains is which path you will choose. Who will win the battle—the natural man or the better one? Frankly speaking, there's nothing more to it than making a conscious decision (or a series of thousands of them).

When presented with an opportunity to shortchange someone, don't. When you could throw someone under the bus to get what you want, choose to lift them up instead. When you want to pick up that bottle of booze, deal with your challenges head-on. When you're tempted to justify not working out, go work out. When you feel like procrastinating on your project, get started on it. When you don't want to have a difficult conversation with someone, decide to get it out of the way. When you want to sit and watch TV, read a book instead.

Look, you don't get self-respect because you want it. You get it because you earn it. It's a battle worth fighting, and it's a battle you can and *must* win.

PURSUE WHAT YOU DESIRE, BUT DO NOT CHASE

There is a huge difference between pursuing what you're after and chasing what you're after. Chasing others and your desires reeks of emotional desperation, whereas pursuing them requires a skilled, disciplined approach to acquiring your target. No man ever earned influence, credibility, and authority by coming across as weak and desperate.

The less a man needs from others, the more attractive he becomes to women, employers, friends, potential clients, etc. The absolute best path to powerful, meaningful connections and the respect that comes with them is to make yourself someone worth partnering with.

That's where self-respect starts—with you. If you truly have the desire to partner with others in different capacities and serve them most effectively, you need to get right with yourself first. The lion does not concern himself with what the gazelle might be doing on a day-to-day basis to improve himself, but you can be certain he is concerned with what he is doing to ensure that he and his pride are going to eat that day.

The path to achieving what you desire starts with you. That's where the emphasis should be placed for two reasons. First, you are the only factor you have control over. You can influence your family, friends, colleagues, and coworkers to make changes in their lives, but you cannot force them to do it. Second, focusing on yourself produces the most effective return for yourself and others. Emphasis on chasing others (as we talked about in Chapter Five, "Don't Be a Hero," when we looked at the concept of the lighthouse versus the tugboat) will produce inferior results compared to becoming a powerful magnet that attracts the right kind of people to you.

Consider what happens when a predator chases his target. It runs. Consider, then, what happens when you chase people and goals. They run from you. Chasing, by definition, means that you are behind what you desire. That isn't where men of influence are situated. Instead, I want you to learn to place a metaphorical ambush on what you desire most. This way, you are not scaring away what you say you want most, but actively and patiently planning for the day opportunities present themselves to you. When they do (and they will), you'll be ready and equipped to maximize your results.

With all of that said, here are three areas you can focus on to develop the self-respect you desire and the level of self-respect others will find irresistible in you.

Train Your Body Daily

Whether you decide to pursue martial arts, strength training, CrossFit, bodybuilding, or simply go for a walk with your family, move and exercise your body daily. Yes, you can find programs and trainers that tell you to exercise two to three times per week, but that's for the average man. You're not average. Or, at least, you're working to rise above being average. Move the machine daily and turn it into the finely tuned instrument it has the potential to become.

Train Your Mind Daily

There are so many opportunities to tap into the most incredible minds the planet has ever known. All you have to do is crack open a book or listen to a podcast, and you unlock access to what our ancestors could only dream of when it comes to information that would have drastically improved their quality of life. Mark Twain said, "The man who does not read has no advantage over the man who cannot read." Don't allow a day to go by without learning something new about yourself, other people, or the world you are inextricably connected with.

Train Your Soul Daily

Training your soul does not merely mean you submit yourself to a higher power (although there is value found in that). When I say "train your soul," I'm encouraging you to get right with yourself mentally, spiritually, and emotionally. It's more about knowing why you're here and what you're meant to do in the grand scheme of things. I've found this is best achieved through a daily meditation, prayer, and/or visualization practice. You can't expect to improve yourself if you don't carve out time every single day to ponder and contemplate how you might do it and what your target even is.

Often, we men place such a heavy emphasis on others. We constantly try to manipulate, coerce, strong-arm, and even force compliance from them. Naturally, your people are going to resist your efforts to do that. Instead of pushing people by chasing them, learn to pull them by becoming someone they're enticed, motivated, and inspired by.

It all starts with you, how you view yourself, and how capable you are of leading others to a place they could not have imagined going on their own. That's when genuine influence kicks in and the desire to chase others around ends.

If you really want to change and lead others, start by changing and leading yourself.

TRAPS AND TACTICS

The level of respect you desire from others starts with the level of respect you have for yourself. No man ever begged his way into gaining influence, authority, and credibility with others. It only comes through making yourself an irresistible force others can't help but be drawn to.

Of course, this is easier said than done, but the fact that it is so elusive for so many men is one of the many reasons you should consider pursuing it for yourself. When you elevate your level of self-respect, you will immediately set yourself apart as unique, compelling, and even somewhat mysterious to those who are drawn to you and those who want to be more like you. This is the foundational source of true influence—a healthy level of respect for yourself physically, mentally, and emotionally.

Fill Your Cup First

We've all heard the same ol' boring instruction when we fly about putting on your own oxygen mask before helping others put on theirs. There's a good reason it's been shared so many times—it's true.

You cannot possibly lead others to a greater capacity than you're willing to lead yourself. And although you may be able to serve others at your own expense for a while, it is truly unsustainable, and you will burn yourself out, which will ultimately undermine the respect you have for yourself and that others have for you.

Make sure you are doing what you need to do to take care of yourself. I can't give you the perfect formula for the amount of time you're spending on your own growth relative to others'; you're going to have to determine that for yourself. But please carve out time for your own personal growth and progress, or you'll stymie everyone else's.

Fill your cup first. I take time every day for myself. I typically give myself time in the morning before everyone is up and time in the evening after everyone is in bed to train Jiu-Jitsu, do my visualization, read a book, research a particular topic, pray, meditate, etc. I've communicated my schedule to those who will be impacted by it, and I stick to it religiously. I make very few exceptions when it comes to filling my own cup. I am better because I do, and so is everyone else.

Don't Become a Punching Bag

If you treat yourself like garbage, you might as well give everyone else express permission to treat you the same way. If, however, you treat yourself as someone worth focusing on, others will be more likely to treat you in kind. The way you treat yourself and allow others to treat you is entirely within your control. Spend a little time thinking about the respect you deserve, draw lines in the sand, communicate those boundaries to others, and enforce them ruthlessly.

If you catch yourself speaking or thinking ill of yourself, replace the script immediately. *DO NOT* treat yourself like a loser, or you'll either consciously or subconsciously act like one. You may feel as if you don't have anything to speak positively about when it comes to your past performance, but that isn't true.

Early on in my financial planning practice, I created an email folder of positive, encouraging emails from clients and friends. In moments of self-flagellation, I would refer to the kind words I had saved from others. Often, it drew me out of my personal pity party and put me back on the path of progress.

Also, do not allow others to speak ill of you. Stand up for yourself, and do not allow yourself to be bullied. You'll find that when you grow a spine, people will respect you more even if they disagree with you about your past performance. Showing others that you are willing and able to defend and respect yourself is a clear indicator of what kind of behavior you expect from them.

And, as a side note, do not allow others to become punching bags. If you see someone else being mistreated, stand up for them. Do not engage in gossip, negativity, and petty nonsense as it relates to other people. Stand up for yourself. Stand up for others. Doing either makes the other more likely.

Don't Be Desperate

Don't become so desperate for the attention, admiration, validation, and/or business of others that you're willing to kick yourself in the proverbial balls to get it. You may need the business or the attention of others, but there are some things that aren't worth what you'd have to give up to get them: your self-respect.

I had a mentor once tell me, "It's important to get yourself noticed in business, but it's also possible to get noticed in the wrong way. Everyone would notice a clown if he were to walk in here right now. No one, however, would have any level of respect for him."

Do not trade a healthy sense of pride and self-worth for a temporary reward you probably won't even care about a few short months from now. Know when to walk away from what you feel you crave. If people don't give you what you want, they're not interested (for myriad reasons). So what? It's okay. You're better off focusing your time and attention on your own growth or serving someone who actually appreciates what you can offer than wasting them on someone who doesn't want or need you.

Ironically, the less desperate you are, the more you'll have in your life. Know where to direct your energy. Know when it isn't appreciated. Be aware of when it isn't producing results. And, like a good steward, invest in only those assets and activities that yield results. Let the rest go.

Have Self-Respect, but Don't Be Arrogant

There's a fine line between self-respect and arrogance. Know where it is, and act accordingly. If you're taking these lessons to heart, your life is, without a doubt, going to improve. People are going to think more highly of you. You're going to think better about yourself. The results you produce are going to improve. Life is going to get better.

But be cautious about buying into your own bullcrap. Just because your life improves does not mean that you're God's gift to the world. It only means you worked an effective formula for self-development and are reaping the inevitable results that come with it.

As quickly as you got results by improving your performance, you can undermine yourself just as quickly. A surefire way to demolish your own performance and self-perception is to let your results go to your head. I've seen an incalculable number of men go through this devastating cycle:

- You do what you need to do to improve your life.
- You gain the admiration, respect, and influence of people in your life.
- You begin to think you're untouchable and all that is right with the world.
- You alienate others because you think you're better than them.
- Your results are diminished because you don't have the support of your team.
- You can't understand why you are so great but can't produce productive results.
- You get bitter and blame your own poor performance on others.
- You hit rock bottom and decide to do something about it.
- You repeat the cycle at step one.

Here's how you keep yourself out of that nonsense: stop thinking you're better than everyone else and learn to pour what you know into others in the same way someone else has likely poured into you. Make your new, improved life about service to others. Remember who you are. Remember where you came from. There's a word for it: humility.

PART IV

LIVE LIKE A MAN

If you can keep your head when all about you
Are losing theirs and blaming it on you . . .
Yours is the Earth and everything that's in it,
And—which is more—you'll be a Man, my son!

—Rudyard Kipling

When I started the Order of Man movement in 2015, I had some real self-doubt about what I wanted this movement to look like and what I ultimately wanted it to become. I also questioned whether I had what it took to bring to life what I envisioned.

At the time, I felt wholly inadequate to suggest to others what it meant to be a man, seeing as how I knew I wasn't living it fully for myself. But I started. I got on the path of manliness. That's what I'm asking you to do—to get on the path.

What I'm *not* asking you to do is to get on my path. What I've outlined within the pages of this book is a path for living a meaningful and fulfilled life as a man. But as with anything, there are an infinite number of ways we can arrive at a similar destination.

See, when I started, I thought it was my purpose to tell anyone who would listen exactly what he should do to become more of a man. But I realize that is not my purpose. Instead, what I know now is that all I can do is share with you the processes, systems, mindsets, and skill sets that have worked for me and the more than three hundred fifty high-caliber men I've had on my podcast. It is not my job to tell you how to live your life. I'm just sharing with you what has worked for so many others, and you can do with it what you will.

In working with thousands of men, I've found that if I make it my sole mission to get you to do what I think you should do, you'll live a life inferior to the one in which you decide what is best for you and yours.

Make no mistake, there are mindsets and characteristics all men inherently possess and are capable of utilizing. That's the what. The how is what you actually do with all that's inside you for yourself and those you're called to lead.

What I've attempted to do throughout this book is lay out a solid framework for personal success and leading others well, and teach you how to establish the influence, authority, and credibility you desire. I think it works. Hell, I know it works because it's the exact process I have used in my life to lose more than fifty pounds; salvage a dying marriage; build a successful financial planning practice; build a thriving men's movement; and, most importantly, step more fully into the role of husband, father, and man.

You now have to decide whether or not you feel it will work for you. If you don't, that's okay. It's my hope that you can take at least some of what I've shared with you and implement it in a way that you see fit. And, if you don't quite know where to start on your own path, try using the mindsets and characteristics I've shared in their entirety.

After everything is said and done, here is what you need to understand: I'm not paying your bills, securing your job promotion, starting your business, managing your health, or building your relationships. That's all on you.

What I think about what you do is irrelevant. My approval of your life, or you as a man, does not matter. But do you know whose approval does? Yours. That's where influence, credibility, and authority start. It starts with the way you view yourself as a man. That takes work.

So, before we close out this book, I want to share with you a few more key concepts to living a rewarding life. The last thing I want to do is tell you all the things I think and give you no clear direction for doing the real work required to thrive as a protector, provider, and presider over yourself and others.

That's one of the problems I have with the self-development space. We've been led to believe that if we're researching a particular subject or reading a book on it, we're moving the needle. We're not. We may be preparing to move the needle, but that's different (important, but different) from actually moving the needle.

In the pages that follow, I'm going to recap what we've discussed and, more importantly, show you how you can create your own manifesto, so to speak. Something that you can refer to often to ensure you're living the type of life you feel you should. It will also serve as a framework for the decisions you make for yourself and others and, ultimately, how you view yourself and show up as a man.

YOUR OWN MANIFESTO

As I stated earlier in this book, I've never been one to mince words, and I don't shy away from discussing what makes a man a man. It's always been my belief that in a world that tells you to reject, put away, and hide what makes you who you are, the man who learns how to embrace and harness it will win.

But you need to own it. You can't own my manifesto any more than you can hope to successfully achieve my goals and desires. They may be aligned, but they are also different in so many ways.

So what I want you to do now is start thinking about what, in this book, really resonated with you, what spoke to you, and what seemed to call to you as the man you could be if you decided to implement the lesson being shared. Equally important is the information I left out of this book and the information I missed that you would have liked to learn more about.

The reality is that I cannot possibly share everything there is to discuss on the subject of men and masculinity, and even if I could, it's likely that you would see many of the conversations and topics quite differently than I do. This is why you'll want to get engaged in the process of defining who you want to be, not simply be a casual reader.

I'd encourage you to get a journal for the following prompts and spend some significant time considering the message I've shared and what you're going to do with it. Answer these prompts in your journal over the next thirty to ninety days. That may seem longer than you think you'll need, but I don't want you to rush it. It's important.

1. What does it mean to be a man?
2. What is the difference between maleness, masculinity, and manliness?
3. How does a man show up differently than a woman?
4. If I were living these ideals, how would I feel about myself?

5. How would people perceive me if I strived to live like the man I described above?

6. What responsibility am I willing to take on in my life?

7. How will I find meaning and purpose in that responsibility?

8. How do I want to show up for others?

9. How do I garner influence, credibility, and authority correctly?

10. What is the proper use of the influence I have with others?

Now, let's talk about the mindsets of masculine leadership. In Part II, I outlined four key mindsets to incorporate in your life and help foster in others that will allow you to lead yourself, your family, your colleagues or coworkers, and your community members most effectively. These are "Overcome the Ease of Modernity," "Don't Be a Hero," "Lead before the Title," and "Render Yourself Obsolete." Now, I want you to think about the mindsets you feel you need to incorporate and develop in others that will allow you to secure the influence, authority, and credibility you need to lead well.

11. What are the mindsets of the great leaders I've had in the past?

12. What are the mindsets of the worst leaders I've had in the past?

13. How do great fathers, husbands, and community leaders show up?

14. What makes a great leader and what motivates/drives him?

15. If I could change one thing about my leadership style, what would it be?

16. How will I know if I'm leading effectively or ineffectively?

17. When someone decides not to follow my lead, how will I respond?

18. What do I want for others? How will I make that happen?
19. What key leadership thought processes did Ryan miss in this book?
20. Where specifically do I agree/disagree with Ryan, and what would I change?

Now that you've addressed the premise of what makes a man a man and how he leads inside the walls of his home, business, and out in his community, let's cover what characteristics you need to foster in order to build out your leadership style effectively. The eight characteristics we covered in the book are stoicism, competitiveness, dominance, aggression, vigilance, violence, honesty, and self-respect. I chose these eight characteristics because I wanted to address some of what society might deem "toxic" or "inherently damaging." That said, I realize there are an infinite number of characteristics you might deem worthy of fostering.

No two leaders are alike, and you aren't required to show up like me or anyone else in order to produce results for you and others. My personality is different from yours. The degree to which we each possess the eight characteristics I shared in Part III vary. The key is to harness who you are, double down on your strengths, shore up your weaknesses, and lead like a man, your way.

21. Which of the eight characteristics resonated most/least with me? Why?
22. Which of the eight characteristics are my strengths/ weaknesses?
23. What characteristics do I possess that were not listed in the book?
24. What do great leaders do? How can I be more like them?
25. What characteristics do I value in others?
26. How will I harness who I truly am to help others?
27. When society attempts to diminish masculine qualities, how will I respond?

28. Do I believe I can be who I have a desire to be? Why or why not?
29. How will I know I'm best utilizing the characteristics that are important to me?
30. How will I adjust my approach to leadership when things are not working correctly?

Armed with the answers to these questions, you will have the self-awareness to step more fully into the man and leader you're meant to become. Most men live their lives by default and never take any amount of time to really contemplate who they are and who they want to become. That's too bad, because you can't expect to change if you're only willing to do what you've always done. If you want more out of your life, you must do more (or do something differently) than you are currently doing.

Once you have spent an appropriate amount of time uncovering the answers to these questions (and the ones you have thought of on your own), I would highly encourage you to turn them into a document that you can refer to often. It's easy to get off track in life. Most men drift with the current of popular culture and the demands and desires of others. That's not leadership, and it does nothing to construct influence, credibility, and authority with others. Learning to be a steadfast, unshakable beacon of light for others does.

Now, you have the foundation in place for making the right moves. Study it. Reflect on it. Update it as needed. But most importantly, *live it*.

NOW, ACT

Congratulations, you've read another book. Now, what are you going to do with all the information I shared with you? I genuinely want to know that not only did you read something that I believe has tremendous potential to positively impact your life and those you'd like to serve, but you *really* took the information to heart and did something with it.

One of my pet peeves is hearing the phrase, "Well, Ryan, that's easier said than done." No shit. It's always easier to talk than it is to do. But that doesn't really improve your surroundings, does it? One other pet peeve of mine is hearing from men how many books they're going to read this year. I once heard a man proudly proclaim that he read two hundred books in 2021. "Two hundred books!" I thought. "How in the world is he going to implement any of that?" The reality is that he is very unlikely to do so.

But I don't want that to be you. Instead of reading two hundred books this year, I'd encourage you to read four to six books and spend the rest of the time implementing and putting into practice the valuable information you acquired. And that's what I'm asking you to do now.

If you completed the previous section (or are still working on it), you've built out your own personal manifesto for the way you want to show up for yourself and others. That's a great starting point. You can't get to where you're going if you don't know where you're starting and what path you're going to take to get there.

What I would suggest that you do now is share your own personal manifesto with those who will be impacted by the decisions you're going to be making—your wife, children, employees, team members, accountability partners, etc. You don't have to disclose personal details you wish to keep private (I wouldn't even recommend that), but you will want to share enough of your manifesto that your family and friends get the gist of what you're trying to accomplish and how you plan on doing it. Remember the discussion of honesty in Chapter Fourteen.

It's likely that, based on what you've read, you will want to start leading a bit differently than you have in the past. Although you may have the best intentions, the change others see in you presents a challenge to their status quo. They may feel intimidated, confused, skeptical, or even threatened by the changes they see in you. That's to be expected. The best way to mitigate their uneasiness is to be honest and forward about who you know yourself to be and how you want to show up for yourself and for them.

What I'd like to share with you now is a very simple three-part formula designed to put what you've learned into practice: visualize, act, review.

The good news is that you already covered the first step with the previous section. That's your vision. The manifesto you drafted is what is going to guide you to make better decisions moving forward. It represents your map when calculating where you are and where you want to go. But having the map is not enough. You must begin your journey.

That's where the second step comes into play. Starting today, I want you to consider exactly *how* you're going to show up in all the places you operate: home, business, community, gym, with buddies, at the game, etc. Then, get to work living out your manifesto.

What principles of leadership guide your decision-making process? How will you serve and inspire others to lead themselves? When things go wrong, how will you handle the situation and yourself?

The key here is to keep that manifesto handy and constantly refer to it to make sure you're on the right track. When you lose your temper, get back on track. When you get frustrated, get back on track. When you feel lost, confused, or alone, get back on track. This leads to the third and final part of this simple formula: review.

Most men are really good at acting. They're good at carrying out their thoughts, for better or worse. But most men are notoriously bad at deciding what those actions should be and having a system in place to ensure they can course correct along the way.

I want you to start each day with your visualization process—your manifesto. And I want you to cap each day with the same. Did you show up for yourself and others the way you wanted to? Did you gain ground or lose ground with others? When you screwed up, how did you correct it (or how should you have)? What are you going to commit to doing better tomorrow? Were you willing to afford others grace on their own journey? Are you willing to afford yourself the same as you strive to become a better man?

One of my favorite quotes is from Gandhi. He said, "Each night, when I go to sleep, I die. And, the next morning, when I wake up, I am reborn."

Allow yourself to die each night. Close the book on the chapter of your day. Don't forget the lessons you learned, but don't carry the baggage from one day into the next. Become a new man each day by killing off the old version of yourself each night.

The three-part formula is an exercise in self-awareness. I believe the greatest leaders—the greatest men—are those who are intimately aware of who they are and who they want to become. I also believe that men who know who they are will always stand as men should and be looked upon by others with the admiration and respect they desire and deserve.

CONCLUSION

As you're well aware, we have a lot of work to do. Not only in society, but in our individual communities, within the walls of our homes, and in our own hearts and minds. It's tempting to believe we ought to look to our external circumstances to make our impact on the world, but it's a mistake to start there.

What I believe we all want as men, in our own way, is to have a positive and lasting impact on the people we care about and to leave a legacy as someone who made a difference. So naturally, we might think that if we can change the external variables, we'll achieve our mission. But there is a better place to begin—with you. Change yourself. Become the man you are meant to be. As you do, you will begin to see the environment respond to the man you're building yourself into.

As I covered the topics of influence, authority, and credibility throughout this book, I began to become concerned that many would interpret my message to mean that we can manipulate others to achieve our desired outcome. That's not correct. That won't help you achieve what you ultimately want.

If anything, using influence, authority, and credibility as tools against the people you care about most will undermine all you're working to create. The bottom line is that influence, authority, and credibility are the inevitable result of the type of man you are. That's it. Simply stated, if you want more, become more.

That is what is required for you, for your family, and for society as a whole—for you and me (and every other man reading this book) to become who we're capable of becoming.

Unfortunately, that is an uphill battle. Much of society would have you believe that you are nothing more than a useful tool as they deem appropriate. Society at large either does not see or refuses to acknowledge that everything within you is not a threat to our way of life but very much the reason for it.

While much of society refuses to acknowledge the incredible role men have played throughout history, they sure don't have any problem enjoying the luxuries afforded by the men they fight so hard against.

Masculinity is not inherently toxic, and it isn't a danger to society. From the time we're little boys, we learn to subdue and suppress the nature of who we are, but I believe the better path is found in uncovering who we are and utilizing our masculinity for the productive outcomes of ourselves and others.

But knowing it's going to be a battle should not deter you from fighting it. Anything worth having is worth fighting for. If you abdicate your responsibility as a man to embrace the work that will serve you and others well, we'll continue to see a decline in the moral decency and prosperity we enjoy. That may be hard for us to see now (in the midst of the greatest abundance the world has ever known), but it's not us who will suffer. It's our children and our grandchildren who will reap the joy or pain of what we sow.

We've all heard G. Michael Hopf's adage that, "Hard times create strong men, strong men create good times, good times create weak men, and weak men create hard times." Where do you think we are in that cycle right now? We're in good times. But let's not be so arrogant to believe that we are the ones who created them. Our ancestors did. And what we do now will determine what those who come after us will experience.

As I said when we started this journey, the responsibility of manliness is a heavy burden to bear. If we are unwilling to bear it, no one will. Besides, there is a tremendous sense of fulfillment and satisfaction found in making yourself capable of dealing with all life has to throw your way and helping others do the same.

The unfortunate reality is that so many men are living a life devoid of meaning. They believe that the sole purpose of life is to find happiness or a state free from worry and toil. And they have the audacity to question why they're financially wealthy but morally broke, surrounded by others but lonelier than they've ever been, blessed but consumed with the quest for the next cheap thrill to hide their misery.

Where most men get lost in the search for sedation, I challenge you to get lost in the search for meaning. It isn't where you want it to be. It's found where you least want it to be. It's found in suffering. It's found in service. It's found in sacrifice.

Know that not only are you capable of shouldering the burden, but you were born to do it. You, after all, were born a male. There is masculinity coursing through your veins. Now, use your birthright to improve yourself, serve your loved ones, and make the world a better place. That is what makes you a man.

THE IRON COUNCIL

In the fall of 2015, I had increasingly found myself dedicating more time to my fledgling little podcast at the expense of my day job—my financial planning practice, Cittica. One night, after dinner and putting the kids to bed, my wife came to me with a look of concern in her eyes.

"Ryan, you're spending a lot of time on this Order of Man thing and spending less and less time with Cittica. I can see you're happy with the direction you're going but you're sacrificing family household income and time away from us," she said. "You should either consider scaling back your time dedicated to Order of Man or find a way to make some money doing it."

I wasn't about to let off the throttle on Order of Man. If anything, I was going to double down.

But she was right. I did have to find a way to turn it into a viable business, not just a hobby, so that I could justify continuing down the path. I had listened to a podcast a few weeks earlier (I can't remember the name of it offhand) and the host and guest suggested the idea of a paid course for members.

Perfect. I didn't know what else to do so I thought I'd start there. I developed a sort of curriculum (I'll explain in a minute) for a twelve-week course for which I would make twelve spots available (myself included). We would focus on six topics I had selected, one every two weeks.

I put together a sales funnel, secured a payment processor, set up a bank account, and promoted it in the Facebook group where we had roughly one thousand members at the time. I called it the Iron Council. We sold out almost immediately.

I remember being thrilled men actually signed up, but also concerned as I hadn't put together the detailed curriculum yet—just the outline of it. *Now I need to go to work!* I thought. It doesn't sound great, but I don't think I would do it any differently if I were to start over.

Eight weeks into the first iteration of the Iron Council, the original twelve members started asking, "What are we going to do when this is over?" Frankly, I hadn't thought about it up to that point. I decided that I would open the Iron Council to more members when the first twelve weeks ended. That was in January 2016.

Since then, the Iron Council has grown to more than 1,500 members throughout the United States and over a dozen other countries. We've poured thousands of hours of research, trial and error, reviews, tweaking, and adjustments into developing the premier men's brotherhood on the planet.

In the darkest days of my life, I found it extremely difficult to find men who were interested in the same level of development I was. It seemed most of them were more interested in the next party, round of golf, or woman than actually working to build long-term impact in their lives.

I realized that if I wanted to have a band of brothers in my life, I was going to have to create an environment for the caliber of men I wanted in my corner to congregate. And since we made that decision over seven years ago, I've been fortunate to not only lead thousands of men towards a better life but drastically improve my own as well. (Sounds like a hair plug commercial—"I'm not only the founder but a client.")

I'm not here to convince you to join the Iron Council. As we discussed through the book, I can't make you do anything, but I might be able to influence you toward something that will, beyond a shadow of a doubt, change your life if you put in the work.

If you are where I was—without a band of brothers in your corner—and you know you are destined and ready for something more out of your life, I'd encourage you to join us. The men who do the work have lost weight, secured promotions, started businesses, salvaged marriages, reconnected with their kids, and, above all, have developed a sense of meaning, fulfillment, and purpose in their lives.

I will spare you the details of what we do inside the Iron Council to help men create these results for themselves. But if you're even remotely interested, I'd encourage you to go to www.orderofman.com/ironcouncil, watch a short video about what we do, and put yourself on the waiting list for the next open registration, which is offered four times per year.

Look, I'm not going to lie to you and say that if you join us all of your wildest dreams will come true. (I'm not running for political office.) Many men join and don't get a single thing out of it. But if you're ready—and I mean truly ready—we'll help you unlock the framework and network needed to thrive and maximize the results from the concepts found in this book.

Again, head to www.orderofman.com/ironcouncil. I hope to see you inside.

ACKNOWLEDGMENTS

I am nothing without my team. Truth be told, I don't particularly enjoy the writing process and I don't consider myself to be a great writer. I wrote this book because its message is crucial for me, you, and the people who support us behind the scenes. It's because of their dedication and diligence that you now have this book in your hand.

I'd like to thank Sandra Smith and Salem Books Editorial Director Karla Dial for poring over the words and concepts in this book. I can't imagine what that must be like. It always sounds pretty good in my head as I read the words to myself. But these great women are the reason the message is as coherent, structured, and refined as it is.

I'd also like to thank Leon Eddards and Todd Van Fleet for making this book look so incredible. They were instrumental in ensuring that the quality of design matched the power of the words I put on paper. As my high school football and baseball coach, Matt Labrum, used to say, "If you look good, you play good." These men made me and this book look good.

Thank you also to the Fedd Agency, specifically Kyle Negrete and Esther Fedorkevich, and to the rest of the team at Salem Books, notably

Publisher Timothy Peterson. I'm not completely sure why you believe in me, but you do. Your generosity, willingness to risk on me, and commitment to the work we're doing here will not be forgotten.

I would also like to express my gratitude for Brandy Cain (who I affectionately refer to as the "murder squirrel"). She has been an incredible friend, a powerful advocate for the work, and instrumental in advancing our mission to reclaim and restore masculinity.

And again, to my wonderful family. I know I was a pain in the rear (more so than normal) for the months I spent hunched over my computer pounding away at the keyboard. You knew how important this was to me and you made it important to yourselves because of it. That is the foundation of family—sacrifice for each other.

Last but not least, to you with this book in your hand, thank you for reading, thank you for believing in Order of Man, and, most importantly, thank you for living as men. Lord knows how much you are needed in the world today.

NOTES

CHAPTER ONE: WHAT MAKES A MAN A MAN

1. "The History of the Lodge," Lodge Cast Iron, https://www.lodgecastiron.com/about-lodge/history.

CHAPTER TWO: THE ARCHETYPE OF MANLINESS: PROTECT, PROVIDE, PRESIDE

1. David Gilmore, *Manhood in the Making: Cultural Concepts of Masculinity* (New Haven, Connecticut: Yale University Press, 1991).
2. Yanna J. Weisberg, Colin G. DeYoung, and Jacob B. Hirsh, "Gender Differences in Personality across the Ten Aspects of the Big Five," *Frontiers in Psychology* 2, no. 178 (August 1, 2011), https://doi.org/10.3389/fpsyg.2011.00178.
3. Louann Brizendine, *The Male Brain: A Breakthrough Understanding of How Men and Boys Think* (New York: Broadway Books, 2010), xvii.
4. Ibid.

CHAPTER THREE: INFLUENCE, AUTHORITY, AND CREDIBILITY

1. Brett Bartholomew, *Conscious Coaching: The Art and Science of Building Buy-In* (CreateSpace, 2017), 266.
2. Ibid.
3. Marianne Williamson, *A Return to Love: Reflections on the Principles of "A Course in Miracles"* (New York: HarperCollins, 1996), 165.

209

PART III: HARNESS MASCULINITY FOR PRODUCTIVE OUTCOMES

1.   Stephanie Pappas, "APA Issues First-Ever Guidelines for Practice with Men and
      Boys," *CE Corner* 50, no. 1 (2019): 34, https://www.apa.org/monitor/2019/01/
      ce-corner.

CHAPTER ELEVEN: AGGRESSION

1.   Notes For Space Cadets, "Jordan Peterson: The Dangers of Being Too
      Agreeable," YouTube, March 29, 2017, https://www.youtube.com/
      watch?v=XVMvQhxN_M8.

CHAPTER THIRTEEN: VIOLENCE

1.   Jocko Podcast, "A Good Man Is Dangerous: Jocko Willink and Jordan
      Peterson," YouTube, 2:59, December 3, 2019, https://www.youtube.com/
      watch?v=xEoVM6iOoXA.
2.   PowerfulJRE, "Joe Rogan Experience #1070—Jordan Peterson," YouTube,
      1:07:45, January 30, 2018, https://www.youtube.com/
      watch?v=6T7pUEZfgdI&t=4066s.